China Briefing

The Practical Application of China Business

For further volumes:
http://www.springer.com/series/8839
http://www.asiabriefingmedia.com

Dezan Shira & Associates is a specialist foreign direct investment practice, providing business advisory, tax, accounting, payroll and due diligence services to multinationals investing in China, Hong Kong, India and Vietnam. Established in 1992, the firm is a leading regional practice in Asia with seventeen offices in four jurisdictions, employing over 170 business advisory and tax professionals.

We also provide useful business information through our media and publishing house, Asia Briefing.

Chris Devonshire-Ellis · Andy Scott
Sam Woollard
Editors

Setting Up Joint Ventures in China

Third Edition

   **DEZAN SHIRA & ASSOCIATES**

Editors
Chris Devonshire-Ellis
Andy Scott
Sam Woollard
Dezan Shira & Associates
Asia Briefing Ltd.
Unit 1618, 16/F, Miramar Tower
132 Nathan Road
Tsim Sha Tsui, Kowloon
Hong Kong, People's Republic of China
e-mail: editor@asiabriefingmedia.com

ISBN 978-3-642-16039-4   e-ISBN 978-3-642-16040-0

DOI 10.1007/978-3-642-16040-0

Springer Heidelberg Dordrecht London New York

Published by Springer-Verlag Berlin Heidelberg
© Asia Briefing Ltd. 2008, 2011

This work is subject to copyright. All rights are reserved, whether the whole or part of the material is concerned, specifically the rights of translation, reprinting, reuse of illustrations, recitation, broadcasting, reproduction on microfilm or in any other way, and storage in data banks. Duplication of this publication or parts thereof is permitted only under the provisions of the German Copyright Law of September 9, 1965, in its current version, and permission for use must always be obtained from Springer. Violations are liable to prosecution under the German Copyright Law.

The use of general descriptive names, registered names, trademarks, etc. in this publication does not imply, even in the absence of a specific statement, that such names are exempt from the relevant protective laws and regulations and therefore free for general use.

Cover design: eStudio Calamar, Berlin/Figueres

Printed on acid-free paper

Springer is part of Springer Science+Business Media (www.springer.com)

About China Briefing's China Business Guides

Thank you for buying this book. China Briefing's publications are designed to fill a niche in the provision of information about business law and tax in China. When we decided, several years ago, to commence this series, we did so in the knowledge that much that was available about China was either expensive, or completely contradictory. Plus much of it did not really adequately address the real issues faced by businessmen—the practical knowledge that must be part of any business dealings in developing countries. This guide is designed to change that perspective and provide detailed information and the regulatory background to business in China—but with a firm eye also on the details of making money and remaining in compliance.

Accordingly, we have made this guide informative, easy to read and inexpensive. To do so we have engaged not a team of journalists or academics—but the services of a respected professional services firm to assist us. The articles and materials within have been researched and written by China-based Chinese and international lawyers, accountants and auditors, familiar with the issues that foreign invested enterprises face in China—as they service them in China as clients. These professionals have come from the nationally established practice, Dezan Shira & Associates, and we are grateful for their support. Without them this book would not have been possible, and we wholeheartedly recommend their services should you require sensible and pragmatic advice as contained within this book.

At China Briefing, our motto is "The practical application of China business" and we hope that within this volume and our other publications you feel we have achieved this, and helped point you in the right direction when it comes to understanding and researching this vast and complicated business environment.

Asia Briefing Publications
Hong Kong

Contents

Devising Your China Investment Strategy 1

Structuring Your JV 23

Development Zones 75

Human Resources 79

China's Business Taxes 87

Joint Venture Conversions and Closures 107

Glossary of Terms 113

Devising Your China Investment Strategy

1 Pre-investment Considerations

If you are contemplating setting up a business in China, you will need to consider what structure to use. But before deciding on the structure, you need to be sure of your strategy—strategy must lead structure. You must first consider why you want to make an investment in China, and find out just what you should be doing, before determining exactly how to do it.

Although a Joint Venture (JV) is no longer the favoured approach in many situations in which foreign investors wish to "go it alone", under some circumstances it can be an ideal structure. In addition, despite widescale liberalization, there are some sectors and areas for which the authorities still insist on a JV structure.

In this initial chapter, then, we will look at how you can decide what structure to choose; explain the structures that are available; introduce the core topic of this book, the Joint Venture; and lay out the key issues you will need to consider when you come to set up the business. In subsequent chapters we will discuss these issues and the establishment process in much more detail.

Why Do You Want to Come to China?

In one of our regional business guidebooks, one contributor outlined the five most common motivations for a new, or increased, China investment. These are:

- *customer pull*—key customer(s) want you to put more resources into China to serve their needs better, and you may need to do so to retain their business
- *attractive market*—there is an identified, incremental market opportunity for your products/services in China

- *competitive threat*—global competitors have a position here which could give them an advantage in cost or proximity to your customer base, and/or local Chinese competitors are starting to penetrate your home market
- *operational efficiencies/cost savings*—moving to China will improve your manufacturing and/or supply chain costs due to proximity to customers/suppliers, lower labor rates, etc.
- *stakeholder push*—there is tangible pressure from your company ownership (board, CEO, stockholders/Wall Street) to become active in China.

There may be several motivational factors in play of course, but almost every China investment boils down to one or more of these. Understanding which applies in your case will help you decide what the correct structure should be.

Equally, when choosing an appropriate investment vehicle, many factors must be considered, as these will lead to different legal and tax considerations. You will need to address questions such as:

- Do you require an entity in Mainland China or is a Hong Kong incorporation sufficient to reach your aims?
- Do you need to invoice locally for services or products?
- Are you getting a feel for the market or have you decided to commit to a larger scale operation?
- Are you planning to set up a production-oriented entity (both for goods or services) or do you need only a representation in the country to carry out market research or liaison activities?
- Will you be involved in trading, manufacturing, services or a combination of these?
- Is the sector you are investing in fully opened to foreign participation or do you still require a local partner?
- Would you need to conduct the business alone, or would you require a Chinese company chipping in with assets or distribution networks?
- Could the foreign enterprise itself carry out the business directly or through the medium of a separate, sometimes unrelated, entity in China?
- Where should you be? You will need to consider issues such as proximity to any China suppliers and raw materials; proximity to any Chinese customers; proximity to ports and other related infrastructure; costs of land and staff; and available incentives.

2 Options Concerning Foreign Investment Vehicles

There are several forms of enterprise from which you can choose. Generally speaking, the most used vehicles include Representative Offices (ROs), Wholly Foreign Owned Enterprises (WFOEs), Foreign Invested Commercial Enterprises (FICEs), and Joint Ventures (JVs). The table shows the differing characteristics of these four structures.

2 Options Concerning Foreign Investment Vehicles

Choosing your China structure

Type of structure	Abbrev.	Legal status	Common purpose(s)	Pros	Cons
Representative office	RO	No legal personality	Market research, planning longer-term ventures, liaison with home country companies	Inexpensive to set up Allows exploration of the market and liaison activity	Cannot invoice locally in RMB Must recruit staff from local agency
Joint venture	JV	Limited liability legal personality (in most cases)	When restrictions require a local partner, or when they can offer e.g. sales and tangible benefits, distribution channels	Use of existing facilities and workforce Use of existing sales/distribution channels Eager to secure long-term export sales	Management can be awkward Inheriting staff liabilities Over inflation of assets or sales in planning Exaggeration of assets or sales by the Chinese partner during JV setup negotiation Technology transfer/IP/management risks Split profits
Wholly foreign owned enterprise	WFOE	Limited liability legal personality	Most manufacturing businesses (for China sales or export), some service businesses	100% Ownership and control More flexible business scope Security of technology/IP Development of own infrastructure Insertion of existing company culture Allowed to convert RMB into foreign currency for profit repatriation	Need to fund total investment capital requirement Development of China sales operations on your own
Foreign invested commercial enterprise	FICE	Limited liability legal personality	WFOE or JV mainly used for trading, distribution, and retail	As for normal WFOEs/JVs (depending on the form of FICE) Specialized structure for trading, retailing and distribution	As for normal WFOEs/JVs (depending on the form of FICE) New structure, implementation/registration process still bedding down

We consider the particular pros and cons of JVs and WFOEs in more detail on the next page. But for the purposes of the rest of this book, we will assume that you have considered these options and decided that a JV is your best bet. For more on ROs and WFOEs, see the relevant books in this series.

What Is a JV and Why Should You Choose It?

A JV is a limited liability company formed by a foreign investor or investors, or a foreign individual, and a Chinese company, in which the foreign party or parties own more than 25% of the shares. Note that a Chinese individual cannot normally be a shareholder in a JV (although they can under some special circumstances—for example, in a JV incorporated in Beijing Zhongguancun High-Tech Park, or as a result of merger or acquisition if the Chinese individual serves as the shareholder of the target company).

We should emphasize—as this point is sometimes misunderstood—that the JV is not a merger between a foreign and Chinese company or companies. The JV is a new entity, partly owned by both sides, in which liability of the shareholders is limited to the assets they brought to the business. Liability does not extend to the parent companies.

There are two types of JVs in China, the Equity JV (EJV) and the Co-operative JV (CJV) (sometimes known as the Contractual JV). They appear similar on the surface but have different implications for the structuring of your entity. This point is not always understood by some of the more rural local governments. We explore the detailed differences between these two types in the next chapter.

Meanwhile, "Joint Venture" sounds a "warm and friendly" way of doing business, doesn't it? A marriage made in heaven, perhaps? You are likely to be offered many such deals. Many Chinese factories are looking for long-term security in foreign sales via an overseas partner, or to get access to western technology. And because this structure has been around for a long time, many foreigners who have not yet done business here have heard about it. It sounds much more attractive conceptually than the main alternative, a Wholly Foreign Owned Enterprise.

But wait! China's business history is littered with thousands of cases of unhappy partnerships and broken dreams—the analogy with human marriage is a common one, with the popular Chinese idiom "same bed, different dreams" often quoted. One major Western oil company once told us, only partly in jest, their JV was a "win–win situation"—meaning the Chinese won twice. Business is not about being "warm and friendly", it is about making profit and running a successful company. You may well end up becoming close friends with a commercial partner, but it is not the primary objective.

You must first ask the question, "why do I need a partner?" They should have something tangible to offer. The first main reason is usually because they can be an entry vehicle into an industrial sector otherwise restricted to 100% foreign investment—the PRC government still requires Chinese company participation or control in some sectors. Alternatively, they are used because they have assets such as a distribution network, brand reputation, a special manufacturing process, or other tangible assets such as land or special licenses.

Using a JV because you think it will lower your cost of market entry in China due to the so-called "shared costs" is a common mistake. It usually does not!

Think also "what does the partner expect or want?" during negotiations, and make sure you take time to understand their perspective, which may not match yours. Sometimes this does not matter, but sometimes it matters very much. As the saying goes, "fools rush in where angels fear to tread". Take your time. Neither China, nor its opportunities, are going away.

Mind you, considering all this, it is no surprise to find that the popularity of JVs has been steadily decreasing. By 2004, JVs accounted for only 32.2 percent of total international investment, compared to 66.4 percent by WFOEs; by the first half of 2010, the WFOE proportion had increased to 77.4 percent, compared to 27 percent in 1995.

On the other hand, it will not end up being zero. In some regions and industries, JVs are still hugely important. For example, in 2005 in Chongqing, 35.3 percent of newly established foreign-invested enterprises (FIEs) were JVs. This reflects the structure of local industry—with many more companies in the restricted sectors—as well as investors' own strategies.

What to Think About When Creating Your JV

Again, remember, strategy must lead structure. It is important to choose to create a JV for the right reasons, as we discussed earlier. But it is equally important to choose the right structure for the JV itself, too, for operational business reasons, not because the legal rules might imply a particular direction.

We will go through these issues in much greater detail in the next chapter, but in the meantime here is a checklist of the issues you will need to consider:

- What will your business scope be? Foreign invested enterprises, and indeed all domestic companies, have to operate within their business scope—this is more critical than in most western countries.
- Is your business in an "encouraged", "permitted", "restricted" or "prohibited" industry for foreign investment? This will determine whether or not you can in fact create a JV, and the incentives available.
- The texts of your "Articles of Association". These will lead you into consideration of issues like board structure, profits repatriation, trade unions, M&A, and liquidation.
- What should be your registered capital and total investment (cash, "in kind", loan etc.)? This is a very important issue, and you will need to focus on it from an operational, not regulatory, point of view—don't be swayed by legal minimums, which may be too low to actually run the business! Your capital needs will be driven by your business model, not the law.

- If you are manufacturing, what proportion of your production is for export, and what for domestic sales? Again, a critical issue with major tax and operational proportion implications—we explain further in subsequent chapters.
- You also need to consider profit distributions and the sharing of responsibility for losses—these can complicate matters in JVs.
- What taxes will you need to pay? These are likely to include business tax, foreign enterprise income tax, VAT, withholding tax, individual income tax, and customs duty—again, we explain more later.
- Where should your company be located? This will depend on your specific sectoral needs, but you may have several options around the country, including possibly several different development zones, with differing characteristics and available incentives.
- Are there any additional issues relating to the specific characteristics of JVs, such as:
    - Who will be the leading party in the daily running of the business?
    - Who will be in charge of sales or export sales?
    - Is it necessary to allow one party to unilaterally increase the registered capital, which would dilute the shares of the other party?

General Establishment Procedures

Different authorities will be involved at different steps of the approval procedure for any foreign entity in China. Throughout the incorporation process you will become more and more familiar with departments like the Administration of Industry and Commerce (AIC), the Bureau of Foreign Trade and Economic Cooperation (BOFTEC) (called Foreign Investment Bureau in some cities), the state and local tax bureaux, the Administrative committees of development zones, customs and so forth.

The establishment procedure involves central, provincial and/or local level authority approvals depending on the sector involved, the amount of the total investment and the location. The Ministry of Commerce (MOFCOM) is the final approval authority for a JV or a WFOE, but it delegates part of its power to its local counterparts, the BOFTEC at provincial and municipality levels. Some specific industries may require additional licensing, which needs to be obtained at the outset.

3 JVs vs WFOEs—Working Out What's Best for You

There are many issues to consider and it can be difficult to be aware of all the implications, especially if you're trying to make this decision based on a few visits (ideally of course you need to spend a fair amount of time in China before committing yourself). Here we explain how to work out the best and most effective route for your China operation—JV or WFOE?

Cash

Many investors think having a JV is a cheaper alternative. That depends, of course! Choosing the JV purely to save money is not a reliable assumption. Capital requirements are usually pretty much the same as a WFOE, and unless the partner can provide, for example, good quality and a well-trained workforce, assuming you'll save money by employing a JV structure is inaccurate. In fact, you may even spend more on management time and the inevitable translation and distance hassles.

Partner's Assets

If you're looking at a JV because your potential partner has assets, then you need to make sure these really belong to him, with no restriction on his property rights, and that they are of good quality. Let's look at three key areas.

Land and Buildings

Usually these are injected into the JV as an asset by the partner. But does he own them? Ask to see a copy of his "land use rights certificate". If he has granted rights in the same name as his business license, he owns the land. If they are "allocated rights", he merely has tenancy. That can affect the security of any development going onto the site, and seriously reduces its value as an asset. You need to know which it is. A valuation should also be taken out to ensure you're being quoted the fair market rate—checks with the local land bureau can reveal this for you, or call in an expert consultant for building valuations.

Equipment

You can do a site visit and are probably in the best position to value the machinery in place in any event. Make an inventory and break it down in detail. We've seen US $20,000 fax machines included! Remember you are essentially buying this so pay attention to detail and ensure prices are fair.

Staff

Be very aware that a JV can inherit the entire welfare history of the staff transferred to it—a neat way for the Chinese side to divest itself of a substantial chunk of liability (and potential hassle) by giving it to their foreign partner. This applies in particular to JVs being formed from State Owned Enterprises (SOEs)—the state employees were guaranteed jobs for life, even if they are transferred to your JV. So be careful who you inherit. We discuss this aspect in more detail in the later HR chapter.

Partners' Intangibles

Often these can be considerable drivers in evaluating the JV option. Make sure they're real!

Sales, Distribution and Logistics

A good intangible to be aware of, but only of value if you want to sell production onto the domestic market. You need to properly evaluate the partner's distribution channels and sales team and ask questions about how it works, where and management issues. Often there can be conflicts—this of course is a major asset to the Chinese and they want to protect this.

So do your homework, ask the questions and if necessary conduct site visits of sale outlets to ensure their product really is out there. Over-inflation of expected sales volumes is rife. Don't get carried away, and make sure it's real.

Technology Transfer

A big, big issue. If you're bringing valuable technology to the JV, will it end up being copied and sold elsewhere? There is no easy answer to this, except to ensure that you know your China market place and make a damage assessment evaluation in the event it does occur. If that is going to have serious implications, then don't go the JV route. No promises or legal protection can help you here. If it's going to happen, it will. Be warned, and if the risk is too high, go a WFOE route—you own it and it's under your control. It's a pure risk assessment issue. Again, we discuss IP in more detail later in the book.

Management

Make sure your partner is totally committed to the project and is motivated by what you bring to the table. If not, there's no point, and if they still want to go ahead it means there is an ulterior motive—usually to your detriment—that is driving them. Remember you also have a company with Chinese management, and maybe personnel you have never worked with before. Do you know who they are? Competencies? If they're on the payroll, check them out and get to see some of their work. You're hiring. Make sure you know who they are.

"Hardly Any JVs Are Successful"

That's an old chestnut. It's also untrue! There are many successful JVs in China, especially those where the dreams of both partners and the business assets match up. Don't listen to the doomwatchers. A lot of JVs say they don't make money. Possibly true. Maybe they are still re-investing their profits. Maybe they want to dissuade the competition.

Maybe to keep the taxman quiet. There is no reason why a JV should not be successful—but it's your responsibility to ensure the tangibles and intangibles are matched up to reduce risk. Bad JVs are the direct result of bad planning and bad management. If that doesn't apply to you, you'll be fine.

Export Opportunities

Many Chinese companies are keen on JVs, because if they are mainly about export sales, then as the country's WTO commitments begin to bite, increased domestic competition means they need to establish a firm base for a secure export market. This is particularly the case as larger domestic firms think about "going global". While this trend is sometimes over-hyped, it is there, and can be a major driver for your local partner.

Finally...Due Diligence

Always conduct due diligence, always take professional advice, and always ensure you've done your homework. Yes, you'll need to hire a consultant, and one with international experience, not the clerk from the local government. Why? Because you need provisions like international distribution of profits, and when was the last time the local officials took any education about that? Both the contract and articles of association need professional drafting, so put aside sufficient funds to get it right, and to get your partner checked out. JVs can work, but do your homework first. False economies are just that.

4 JV Regulatory Issues and Implementing Rules

The fundamental legal basis for JVs varies depending on whether they are EJVs or CJVs. For CJVs, it is the *Law of the People's Republic of China on Sino-foreign Cooperative Enterprises*, promulgated on April 13, 1988, and revised October 31, 2000.

The relevant implementing regulations are the *Regulations for the Implementation of the Law on Sino-foreign Cooperative Enterprises*, promulgated on September 4, 1995. These are lengthy and the full text is available on request from info@dezshira.com.

Meanwhile for EJVs, the relevant statute is the *Law of the People's Republic of China on Sino-foreign Equity JVs*, promulgated on July 1, 1979, and amended in April 1990 and March 2001.

The relevant implementing regulations are the *Regulations for the Implementation of the Law of the PRC on JVs using Chinese and Foreign Investment*, promulgated on September 20, 1983, and revised in January 1986, December 1987 and July 2001. These are lengthy and the full text is available on request from info@dezshira.com.

On occasion, these need to be read in conjunction with the *Company Law*, the most recent version being that which became effective January 1, 2006.

http://english.mofcom.gov.cn/aarticle/policyrelease/internationalpolicy/200703/20070304466100.html.

Article 218 of this states:

"The limited liability companies and joint stock companies invested with foreign investment shall be governed by this law. Where the laws for foreign investment enterprises have other provisions, such other provisions shall be applicable".

In other words:

- the JV law prevails
- but if the JV law is silent on an issue, the Company Law applies.

The full text of the JV laws can be found below.

Law on Sino-foreign Cooperative Joint Ventures

(Adopted April 13, 1988 at the 1st Session of the 7th National People's Congress. Amended October 31, 2000 at the 18th Meeting of the Standing Committee of the National People's Congress by the Decision on the Revision of the Law of the People's Republic of China on Sino-foreign Co-operative Enterprises)

Article 1. This Law is formulated in order to expand economic co-operation and technological exchange with foreign parties and to encourage foreign enterprises and other economic entities or individuals (hereinafter referred to as foreign partners) to establish joint Sino-foreign co-operative enterprises (hereinafter referred to as co-operative enterprises) within Chinese territory together with enterprises or other economic entities of the People's Republic of China (hereinafter referred to as Chinese partners) in accordance with the principles of equality and mutual benefit.

Article 2. When Chinese and foreign partners establish a co-operative enterprise, provisions on such items as investment or terms for co-operation, distribution of earnings or products, sharing of risks and losses, method of business management and the ownership of property on the expiry of the contract term shall be prescribed in the co-operative enterprise contract in accordance with the provisions of this Law.

A co-operative enterprise, which complies with the provisions of Chinese law for a legal person, shall acquire the status of a Chinese legal person.

Article 3. The State shall protect the legal rights and interests of co-operative enterprises as well as the Chinese and foreign partners in accordance with the law.

A co-operative enterprise shall abide by the laws and regulations of the People's Republic of China and shall not harm the public interests of Chinese society.

The relevant State organs shall supervise co-operative enterprises in accordance with the law.

Article 4. The State shall encourage the establishment of export-oriented or technologically advanced production-type co-operative enterprises.

Article 5. When applying to establish a co-operative enterprise, the agreement, contract, articles of association and other relevant documents signed by the Chinese and foreign partners shall be submitted for examination and approval to the State Council department in charge of foreign economic relations and trade or a department or local government authorized by the State Council (hereinafter referred to as an examining and approving organ). The examining and approving organ shall make a decision on whether or not to approve the application within 45 days of its receipt.

Article 6. Following approval of an application to establish a co-operative enterprise, an application for registration and a business license shall be made to the administration for industry and commerce within 30 days of receiving the certificate of approval. A co-operative enterprise shall be deemed to be established from the date of issue of its business license.

A co-operative enterprise shall register with the taxation organ for tax purposes within 30 days of its establishment.

Article 7. If, during the term of co-operation, the Chinese and foreign partners agree through consultation to make a major amendment to the co-operative enterprise contract, the matter shall be reported to the examining and approving organ for approval. If the amendment involves items for official industrial or commercial registration or tax registration, procedures for registration of the amendment shall be conducted with the administration for industry and commerce or the taxation organ.

Article 8. Investment or terms for co-operation by Chinese and foreign partners may be in the form of cash, kind, land-use rights, industrial property rights, non-patented technology and other property rights.

Article 9. The Chinese and foreign partners shall discharge their obligations both to subscribe their investment in full and to provide conditions for co-operation on schedule, in accordance with the provisions of the laws and regulations and the provisions agreed on in the co-operative enterprise contract. In the event of failure to fulfill such obligations, the administration for industry and commerce shall stipulate a deadline for fulfillment and, if obligations are still not fulfilled by the stipulated date, the examining and approving organ and the administration for industry and commerce shall handle the matter in accordance with the relevant regulations.

The investment or terms for co-operation to be contributed by Chinese and foreign partners shall be examined and verified by an accountant registered in China or a relevant organ and a certificate shall be issued.

Article 10. If any one party to a Sino-foreign co-operation wishes to assign, in full or in part, its rights and liabilities as prescribed in the co-operative enterprise contract, the agreement of the other party shall be obtained and the matter shall be reported to the examining and approving organ for approval.

Article 11. A co-operative enterprise shall conduct business management activities in accordance with the approved co-operative enterprise contract and articles of association and its right of autonomy in the area of business management shall not be interfered with.

Article 12. A co-operative enterprise shall set up a board of directors, or a joint management body, to make decisions on major issues involving the co-operative enterprise in accordance with the provisions of the co-operative enterprise contract or articles of association. One party of the Chinese and foreign partners shall appoint a person to hold the position of chairman of the board of directors or head of the joint management body and a person appointed by the other party shall hold the position of deputy chairman of the board of directors or deputy head. The board of directors or the joint management body may decide on the appointment or engagement of a general manager to conduct the daily business management of the co-operative enterprise. The general manager shall be responsible to the board of directors or the joint management body.

After the establishment of a co-operative enterprise, if a party other than the Chinese and foreign partners is engaged to manage the business, the unanimous agreement of the members of the board of directors or the joint management body must be obtained. The matter shall be reported to the examining and approving organ for approval and the change shall be registered with the administration for industry and commerce.

Article 13. Matters such as the recruitment and dismissal of employees, remuneration, welfare benefits, labor protection and labor insurance shall be stipulated in contracts signed in accordance with the law.

Article 14. Co-operative enterprise employees shall abide by the law in establishing a trade union organization for the promotion of trade union activities and the protection of their legal rights and interests.

A co-operative enterprise shall provide its enterprise trade union with the necessary facilities for its activities.

Article 15. A co-operative enterprise shall establish books of account within the territory of the People's Republic of China, shall submit accounting statements in accordance with regulations and shall accept supervision by the financial and taxation organs.

If a co-operative enterprise violates the provisions of the previous paragraph and does not establish books of account within the Chinese territory, the taxation organ may issue a fine and the administration for industry and commerce may order the closure of operations or may revoke the business license of the co-operative enterprise.

Article 16. A co-operative enterprise shall present its business license and open a foreign exchange account with a bank or other financial institution authorized by an organ of the State Administration of Exchange Control to engage in foreign exchange dealings.

The foreign exchange dealings of a co-operative enterprise shall be handled in accordance with the relevant State provisions on exchange control.

Article 17. A co-operative enterprise may obtain a loan from a financial institution within Chinese territory or from overseas.

Any loan and the loan guarantee raised by a Chinese or foreign partner for investment or for a contractual provision shall be arranged by the respective party.

Article 18. The various kinds of insurance required by a co-operative enterprise shall be furnished by an insurance organization within Chinese territory.

Article 19. A co-operative enterprise may, within its approved scope of operations, import goods and materials it requires and export the resulting manufactured products. A co-operative enterprise may, within its approved scope of operations and in accordance with the principle of fairness and reasonableness, purchase raw materials, fuel and other requirements from both domestic and international markets.

Article 20. A co-operative enterprise may also enjoy favorable treatment in the form of a reduction of or exemption from tax payments, following its payment of taxes due in accordance with the relevant State regulations.

Article 21. Chinese and foreign partners shall distribute income or products and shall bear the responsibility for risks or losses in accordance with the provisions stipulated in the co-operative enterprise contract.

When the Chinese and foreign partners agree in the co-operative enterprise contract that, on the expiry of the duration of the term of co-operation, all the fixed assets of the co-operative enterprise shall revert to ownership by the Chinese partner, methods to allow the foreign partner to recover its investment within the term of co-operation may be stipulated in the co-operative enterprise contract.

If a co-operative enterprise contract stipulates that the foreign partner shall recover its investment before paying income tax, an application shall be submitted to the finance and taxation organs which shall examine and determine an approval of the matter in accordance with the relevant State provisions on taxation.

When the foreign partner recoups its investment within the period of co-operation according to the provisions of the previous paragraph, the Chinese and foreign partners shall be responsible for the liabilities of the co-operative enterprise in accordance with the provisions of the relevant laws and the stipulations of the co-operative enterprise contract.

Article 22. Dividends remaining after a foreign partner has fulfilled all obligations as prescribed in the laws and regulations and the stipulations of the co-operative enterprise contract, and other legal income and funds distributed by the co-operative enterprise at the termination of co-operation may be remitted abroad in accordance with the law.

Income in the form of wages or other legal earnings of employees of foreign nationality of a co-operative enterprise may be remitted abroad after payment of individual income tax in accordance with the law.

Article 23. On the expiry or premature termination of the term of a co-operative enterprise, assets, claims and debts shall be liquidated in accordance with legal procedures. Chinese and foreign partners shall determine ownership of co-operative enterprise property in accordance with the stipulations of the co-operative enterprise contract.

On the expiry or premature termination of the term of a co-operative enterprise, the procedures for the cancellation of registration shall be carried out with the administration for industry and commerce and the taxation organ.

Article 24. The duration of the term of co-operation of a co-operative enterprise shall be determined through a consultation by the Chinese and foreign partners and specified in the co-operative enterprise contract. If the Chinese and foreign partners agree to extend the term of co-operation, an application shall be submitted to the examining and approving organ 180 days before the expiry of the term of co-operation. The examining and approving organ shall decide whether or not to approve the application within 30 days of receipt.

Article 25. If a dispute arises between Chinese and foreign partners over the implementation of a co-operative enterprise contract, the matter shall be resolved through consultation or mediation. If the Chinese and foreign partners are unwilling to use consultation or mediation to resolve the dispute or if consultation or mediation fail to produce a result, the matter may be submitted to a Chinese arbitral body or another arbitral body for arbitration in accordance with the provisions on arbitration in the co-operative enterprise contract or an arbitral agreement concluded in writing after the dispute has arisen.

If the Chinese and foreign partners have not included provisions on arbitration in the co-operative enterprise contract and fail to conclude a written arbitral agreement after a dispute has arisen, a suit may be filed in a Chinese court.

Article 26. The State Council department in charge of foreign economic relations and trade shall formulate implementing rules in accordance with the provisions of this Law, to be implemented following their approval by the State Council.

Article 27. This Law shall take effect from the date of promulgation.

Law on Sino-foreign Equity Joint Ventures

(Adopted July 1, 1979 at the 2nd Session of the 5th National People's Congress. Amended April 4, 1990 at the 3rd Session of the 7th National People's Congress in accordance with the Decision to Revise the Law of the People's Republic of China on Sino-Foreign Equity Joint Ventures. Amended March 15, 2001 at the 4th Session of the 9th National People's Congress in accordance with the Decision to Revise the Law of the People's Republic of China on Sino-Foreign Equity Joint Ventures.)

Article 1. In order to expand international economic co-operation and technological exchange, the People's Republic of China shall permit foreign companies, enterprises and other economic entities or individuals (hereinafter referred to as foreign partners) to establish, within the territory of the People's Republic of China, equity joint ventures with Chinese companies, enterprises or other economic entities (hereinafter referred to as partners), in accordance with the principles of equality and mutual benefit, subject to the approval by the Chinese government.

Article 2. The Chinese government, pursuant to the provisions of agreements, contracts and articles of association which it has approved, shall protect foreign partners' investment in equity joint ventures, profits due to them and their other legal rights and interests in accordance with the law.

All activities of an equity joint venture shall be governed by the laws and regulations of the People's Republic of China.

The state shall not subject equity joint ventures to nationalization or expropriation in special circumstances, however, in order to meet public interest requirements, the State may expropriate an equity joint venture in accordance with the legal procedures, but certain compensation must be paid.

Article 3. Equity joint venture agreements, contracts and articles of association to which the various parties to an equity joint venture are signatories shall be submitted to the state department in charge of foreign economics and trade (hereinafter referred to as an examining and approval authority) for examination and approval. An examining and approval authority shall decide whether or not to grant the approval within 3 months. Once approved, an equity joint venture shall register with a state administration for industry and commerce after obtaining a business license.

Article 4. An equity joint venture shall take the form of a limited liability company.

The proportion of investment contributed by a foreign partner as its share of the registered capital of an equity joint venture shall in general be no less than 25%.

Equity joint venture partners shall share profits and bear risks and losses in proportion to their contribution to the registered capital of an equity joint venture.

The transfer of one party's share of the registered capital shall be effected only with the consent of the other parties to the equity joint venture.

Article 5. Each party to an equity joint venture may contribute cash, capital goods, industrial property rights, etc., as its investment in the enterprise.

Technology and equipment contributed as investment by a foreign partner must genuinely be advanced technology and equipment appropriate to China's needs. If losses occur due to deception resulting from the intentional supply of outdated technology or equipment, compensation shall be paid.

The investment contribution of a Chinese partner may include providing site-use rights for an equity joint venture during its period of operations. If site-use rights are not part of the Chinese partner's investment contribution, the equity joint venture shall be required to pay site-use fees to the Chinese government.

The various items of investment mentioned above shall be specified in the equity joint venture contract and articles of association. The value of each item (excluding the site) shall be determined by the equity joint venture partners through joint assessment.

Article 6. An equity joint venture shall establish a board of directors composed of a certain number of members determined through consultation by the equity joint venture partners and stipulated in the equity joint venture contract and articles of association. Each equity joint venture partner shall be responsible for the appointment and replacement of its own directors. The chairperson and deputy chairperson shall be selected by the equity joint venture partners through consultation or shall be elected by the board of directors. Where the chairperson is appointed from one party to an equity joint venture, the deputy chairperson shall be appointed from the other party. The board of directors, in accordance with the principles of equality and mutual benefit, shall decide all the important matters of an equity joint venture.

A board of directors is empowered to discuss and take action on, pursuant to the provisions of the articles of association of the equity joint venture, all the important issues concerning the enterprise, namely, enterprise development plans and production and operational projects, its income and expenditure budget, profit distribution, labor and wage plans and suspension of operations; as well as the appointment or hiring of the general manager, deputy general manager, chief engineer, chief accountant and auditor, and determining their functions and powers, remuneration, etc.

The general and deputy general managers (or general and deputy factory heads) shall be appointed separately by each of the joint venture partners.

Matters such as the recruitment, dismissal, remuneration, welfare benefits, labor protection and labor insurance of employees of an equity joint venture shall be stipulated in contracts concluded in accordance with the law.

Article 7. Employees of an equity joint venture may establish a trade union organization according to the law for the promotion of trade union activities and the protection of the legal rights and interests of employees.

An equity joint venture shall provide its enterprise trade union with the necessary facilities for its activities.

Article 8. After payment of equity joint venture income tax on an enterprise's gross profit, pursuant to the tax laws of the People's Republic of China, and after deductions there from as stipulated in its articles of association regarding reserve funds, employee bonus and welfare funds and enterprise development funds, the net profit of an equity joint venture shall be distributed between the equity joint venture partners in proportion to their investment contribution to the enterprise's registered capital.

An equity joint venture may enjoy preferential treatment in the form of tax reductions or exemptions in accordance with the provisions of the relevant state tax laws and administrative regulations.

A foreign partner that reinvests its share of an equity joint venture's net profit within the Chinese territory may apply for a rebate on that portion of income tax already paid.

Article 9. An equity joint venture shall present its business license to a bank or other financial institution authorized by a state exchange control organ to engage in foreign exchange dealings and shall open a foreign exchange account.

An equity joint venture shall conduct its foreign exchange transactions in accordance with the Regulations of the People's Republic of China for Foreign Exchange Control.

An equity joint venture may, in its business operations, obtain funds directly from foreign banks.

The various items of insurance required by an equity joint venture shall be furnished by insurance companies within the Chinese territory.

Article 10. An equity joint venture, within its approved scope of operations and in accordance with the principles of fairness and reasonableness, may purchase raw materials, fuels, and other such materials from both domestic and international markets.

An equity joint venture shall be encouraged to sell its products outside China. It may sell its export products on foreign markets through its own direct channels or its associated agencies or through China's foreign trade establishments. Its products may also be sold on the domestic Chinese market.

If deemed necessary, an equity joint venture may establish branch organizations outside China.

Article 11. Net profit received by a foreign partner after executing obligations prescribed by the relevant laws, agreements and contracts, funds received on the termination or suspension of an equity joint venture's operations and other relevant funds may be remitted abroad in accordance with the exchange control regulations and in the currency specified in the equity joint venture contract.

A foreign partner shall be encouraged to deposit in the Bank of China foreign exchange that it is entitled to remit abroad.

Article 12. Wage income and other legitimate income earned by equity joint venture employees of foreign nationality may be remitted abroad in accordance with the exchange control regulations after payment of individual income tax pursuant to tax laws of the People's Republic of China.

Article 13. The duration of an equity joint venture's term of operations may differ, depending on the line of business and other differing circumstances. The term of operations must be set for some types of equity joint ventures, while for other types of equity joint ventures, the setting of the term of operations is optional. In the case of an equity joint venture which has its term of operations set, the term may be extended subject to the agreement of all equity joint venture partners and the lodging of an application with the examining and approval authority 6 months before the expiry of the joint venture term. The examining and approval authority shall decide whether to approve or reject an application within 1 month of its receipt.

Article 14. In the event that an equity joint venture incurs heavy losses, or a party fails to execute its obligations as prescribed in the equity joint venture contract or articles of association, or an event of force majeure occurs, etc., the contract may be terminated subject to the negotiation and agreement reached by all parties of an equity joint venture, the approval of the examining and approval authority and registration with the State Administration for Industry and

Commerce. If a loss is incurred due to a breach of contract, the party that violated the contract provisions shall bear the financial liability for the loss.

Article 15. Any dispute arising between equity joint venture partners that the board of directors is unable to settle through consultation may be resolved through conciliation or arbitration by a Chinese arbitral body or through arbitration conducted by an arbitral body agreed on by all parties of an equity joint venture.

If the parties of an equity joint venture have not stipulated an arbitration clause in their contract or do not reach a written arbitration agreement after a dispute has arisen, they may file a lawsuit in a people's court.

Article 16. This Law shall take effect from the date of promulgation.

5 Encouraged Industry Applications

You will also need to determine the official status of your industry sector, and thus whether or not you need some form of Chinese involvement as a JV partner, or whether you can in fact "go it alone" with a WFOE. To do so, you should refer to the so-called Catalogues – there are two different documents, the first is the Catalogue for the Guidance of Foreign Investment Industries, which applies to the whole of China, the second is the Catalogue of Priority Industries for Foreign Investment in the Central-Western Region.

The Catalogue for the Guidance of Foreign Investment was published by the National Development and Reform Commission (NDRC) and the Ministry of Commerce. It categorizes different industries in China as "encouraged," "permitted," "restricted," and "prohibited" to foreign investment. These categories are defined as follows:

- "permitted"—any industry not listed in the other categories is "permitted"
- "encouraged"—these include sectors that promote the development of agriculture, involve high technology, upgrade product quality, promote environmental protection, promote exports and which will help in the development of the poorer and less-developed interior regions – these sectors get some special incentives
- "restricted"—these industries include those that are technologically backward, environmentally unfriendly or industries that are being opened up to foreign investment on a pilot basis
- "prohibited"—these industries are those that use technology unique to China or, not surprisingly, which harm the national interest, are damaging to the environment or human health, jeopardise security or are politically sensitive

Certain industries under both the "encouraged" and "restricted" categories are only open to Sino-foreign joint venture enterprises or other entities with a limited percentage of foreign investment. The latest version of the catalogue was published in 2007. An English version of the 2007 edition can be obtained on request from info@dezshira.com.

On April 1, 2011, the Legislative Affairs of the State Council published the draft 2011 Catalogue for the Guidance of Foreign Investment Industries for public comments. The comment period ended on April 30, 2011 and the draft is expected to be adopted in the next quarter.

The draft 2011 Foreign Investment Catalogue added more environmentally-friendly and high-end projects to the "encouraged" category, including new materials deemed to be environmentally-friendly, automotive parts and components that result in energy savings, environmentally-friendly battery manufacturing technology, the construction of water recycling facilities, and investment in charging facilities for electric vehicles. Other industry sectors and products/services, including aviation, aerospace, light motorcycles, advanced generation equipment for Internet and network systems, advanced semi-conductor development, and exploration and exploitation of unconventional natural gas resources, were also included in the "encouraged" category.

The draft Catalogue also reflects China's desire to further restrict projects that require heavy energy consumption or cause elevated levels of pollution, as well as to impose stricter controls on its housing bubbles by prohibiting foreign investment in the construction and operation of villas.

The latest version of the Catalogue of Priority Industries for Foreign Investment in the Central-Western Region was published in 2008 and entered into force on January 1, 2009, replacing the 2004 version of the catalogue as well as the 2006 Catalogue of Priority Industries for Foreign Investment in Liaoning Province. The catalogue contains a total of 411 priority industries in 21 provinces and autonomous regions in the central and western regions, i.e., Shanxi, Jilin, Heilongjiang, Anhui, Jiangsu, Henan, Hubei, Hunan, Chongqing, Sichuan, Guizhou, Yunnan, Tibet, Shaanxi, Gansu, Qinghai, Ningxia, Xinjiang, Inner Mongolia, Guangxi and Liaoning. Unlike the Catalogue for the Guidance of Foreign Investment Industries, this catalogue contains only priority industries, and all projects listed in the catalogue enjoy preferential policies applied towards foreign investment in the "encouraged" sectors, including the ability to obtain custom duty exemption on imported equipment.

Currently, the lion's share of FDI remains in manufacturing, but significant amounts are starting to drift into services and the tertiary sector, and indeed into the primary sector, as more areas are opened up and the economy becomes more sophisticated.

Applying for "Encouraged" Status

As with all business applications, these first need to go to the Ministry of Commerce or its regional office for the Approval Certificate, then to the regional office again for the business licence. For encouraged status applications, these now need to be approved by the National Development and Reform Commission.

It is worth noting that—as in many cases in China—officials do appear to apply some administrative discretion to the definitions within these categories. For example, we have been able to negotiate cases where a manufacturer wished to manufacture product A, but this was not in an "encouraged" industry. However, a by-product of their process, product B, was in an "encouraged" industry. It proved possible to frame their business scope around product B, not product A and therefore obtain encouraged industry status.

NDRC issued a notice FGWZ [2006] No. 316 on February 22, 2006 to provide more details on certification procedures for encouraged projects, define more clearly who the responsible approving authorities are, and warn against abuses.

Major points of the notice are as follows:

- for a foreign invested project with total investment over US$30m, the project approval paper should be issued by NDRC.
- for projects under US$30 million, the project approval papers should be issued by a Provincial Development and Reform Commission.
- no entities other than NDRC or its provincial agencies have authority to issue the approval paper.

The procedures apply both to initial approval of Sino-foreign Equity JVs (EJVs), Sino-foreign cooperative JVs (CJVs) and wholly foreign-owned enterprises (WFOEs), and increases in total investments of existing EJVs, CJVs and WFOEs. Further filings for tax exemption on imported goods need to be made with the customs and tax bureaus.

The notice also emphasizes that a project with total investment in excess of US$30 million cannot be "compartmentalized" to avoid the scrutiny of the NDRC.

Similarly FIEs are warned that they must not understate the amount of total investment and apply for an increase after a project and corresponding exemption are approved. Applicants and local approving agencies are also warned against unwarranted "stretching" of the meaning of exempt criteria. NDRC says it would strengthen review of approvals granted in respect of projects below US$30m to identify irregularities. Violations may lead not only to withdrawal of exemption, but also disruption of importation and hence serious financial damages to those involved.

If a WFOE applies to be evaluated as "encouraged sector" after its establishment, such as in the case with an alteration or addition to its scope of business, or in the event this had previously been overlooked, the company would need to supply the following documents to the authorities:

- application form.
- copy of Business License.
- Feasibility Study Report.
- Certificate of Approval.
- list of imported machinery and equipment with description of number, unit price, total price.

5 Encouraged Industry Applications 21

If the application involves an increase of capital, an audit report should also be submitted to the original approval authority.

6 Conclusion

It is important to be aware if your intended activities in China fall into the "encouraged" sector. If so, and you or your advisors are aware of this, your company may apply for significant benefits in the reduction of tax. However, if you are not aware of these benefits and do not make a specific application to apply for them—your business stands to lose out significantly in terms of saved revenues.

Structuring Your JV

So you have decided to set up a JV. Now what? You need to work on the structure. In this chapter we will look at the issues surrounding the setting-up of JVs, as well as due diligence on partners, and the agreement, contracts and articles of association.

Establishing entities of all kinds in China is a relatively straightforward procedure, if you know what you are doing. It is, however, certainly not an "off the shelf" administrative application and the completion of a few sheets of paper. JVs, especially, need a lot of care and attention to detail. You need to put careful thought into the negotiations and application, and consider a number of serious operational issues.

1 Structuring Joint Ventures: General Issues

There are several major, inter-related issues to address if you intend to set up a JV in China. Some of the issues you need to consider apply to all types of foreign entities in China, while others relate specifically to JVs.

- Business scope—what should yours be?
- Registered capital requirements—these may vary depending on the industry and the location. It is also absolutely critical that you do not simply put in the minimum because the regulations say you can—you may find the business is under-capitalized if you do so. This is an operational judgment for you, not the bureaucrats.
- Are you manufacturing 100% for export, or part for export, part for domestic sales? Where are your clients located? Do they require an official local invoice? Would they require you to sell your goods to Hong Kong or other off-shore jurisdictions? This has a fundamental impact on how you structure the business!

- Agreement, contract and articles of association—these need detailed work by you to ensure you cover all the bases. You are setting up a company with a 20–30 year life span and you need to be sure you know what you are getting into.

We will now explore these in more detail.

Business Scope

Having set up a limited company does not necessarily mean you can engage in any kind of business activity, as is the case in some western countries. Like other entities in China, JVs can only be operated within the business scope approved by the authorities. Other activities are subject to further approval. So it is vital to determine what you want to do right from the start.

Lazy, or deliberately disingenuous, business scopes, such as only using the phrase "production of (product)", will not necessarily qualify a JV as a production company. We have encountered numerous problems of this nature, all requiring a scope of business change on the license before the tax bureau is satisfied. You need to ensure your business scope is accurate. Attempts to fool the tax bureau into thinking you are one thing, while in fact you are another—even if you can get it past the approvals process—inevitably end in failure. Play the game and say what it is you are really doing.

Registered Capital Requirements: Avoiding Under-Capitalization Miseries

One of the most common, and most serious, problems with WFOE applications, especially for small businesses, is the issue over registered capital. This is a much misunderstood area. Confusion exists, and many ill-advised investments are made due to misinterpretation of the local governments term "minimum registered capital". It is not supposed to be a ruling on how much you need to invest. Registered capital is the initial investment in the company that is immediately used in its operation—part of the "working capital" if you like. Get this wrong and it is financially painful to change it.

The official requirements vary from industry to industry, and also on a regional basis. A WFOE wanting to establish in Beijing may face different capital requirements than one in Tianjin, Shanghai or Dongguan. Also, some regions have their own regional incentive policies encouraging foreign investment and require lower registered capital.

So, if you can be flexible on location, shop around and compare regional differences. With much of China's eastern and southern coastal areas possessing sound import-export infrastructure, it may be more efficient to place the factory in one of the second-tier cities—capital requirements and operating costs vary quite considerably. Additionally, there is often conflict here between the local government—keen on securing another foreign investor in order to meet its targets—and other government departments, responsible for monitoring and managing China business issues, especially the tax bureau and customs.

It is important to note that tax collection is administered centrally, while the approvals process is at a local level. This means conflicts can and do arise between what the local government says in order to attract your investment, and what the tax bureau then says in dealing with any lack of compliance. And by then it's too late—you are already committed—and you have no choice other than to go through additional pain and hassle to get things put right, usually involving more investment.

In fact, some local government officials are downright reckless when using "minimum registered capital requirements" as a sales pitch. The amounts they state may not be in compliance with the actual needs of businesses or other government department requirements—the classic obfuscation that so often blurs the thinking and otherwise competent planning by international investors. There are also many, many consultants out there who are also either blissfully unaware and ignorant of the real importance of registered capital and how to cater for it properly, or downright calculating, knowing that under-capitalisation can drive additional business their way from the unfortunate investor if they play the scenario correctly.

So why are there capital requirements? the authorities use capital as an entry barrier to ensure FIEs are of the relevant quality and financial strength in addition, such rules protect suppliers and others involved in the company's business from incurring any liability.

Wherever you site your WFOE, however, basic investment criteria remain the same, the government will look at the general viability of the project and a reasonable cash requirement for a particular type of investment. Injections of cash and plant only take place after the WFOE licence is approved, so it is a no-risk investment in terms of money up-front.

Registered capital and total investment figures are both required to be specified in the Feasibility Study Report and the WFOE's Articles of Association before the approval certificate is issued. Unlike registered capital, which has to be fully paid into the WFOE's Chinese bank account before starting business operations, the total investment quota is the total amount of funds planned to be contributed to the project over its lifespan and it does not necessarily have to be fully deposited in the bank account.

The Provisional Rules on the Ratio between Registered Capital and Total Investment of Sino-foreign Equity Joint Venture Enterprises applies to the registered capital and total investment ratio of all foreign-invested enterprises, including WFOEs. The mandated ratio is expressed in the table below:

3 Million or below	7/10 of the Total Investment
Over 3 Million and under 4.2 Million	2.1 Million
4.2 Million to 10 Million	1/2 of the Total Investment
Over 10 Million and under 12.5 Million	5 Million
12.5 Million to 30 Million	2/5 of the Total Investment
Over 30 Million and under 36 Million	12 Million
36 Million or above	1/3 of the Total Investment

The difference between registered capital and total investment represents the debt of the investment and can be made up by loans from the investor or foreign banks. Pay attention to the relationship between registered capital and total investment in case you need to obtain further debt or other financing from your holding company or other financial institution. Keeping this window open will cost you nothing, but closing yourself off from further financing by equating registered capital and total investment may leave you handcuffed. The payment schedule of the WFOE registered capital also needs to be specified in the Articles of Association. The investor may choose to pay it as a lump sum or in installments.

Registered Capital: How Much is Enough?

So how much do you have to pay? Under the New Company Law, which came into force on January 1, 2006, absolute minimum capital requirements are:

- for multiple shareholder companies RMB30,000 (article 26)
- for single shareholder companies RMB100,000 (article 59).

However, in terms of foreign-invested companies, these figures are very misleading. Article 26 of the Law also states, "if any law or administrative regulation prescribes a relatively higher minimum amount of registered capital of a limited liability company, the provisions of that law or administrative regulation shall be followed".

For example, some specific cases of registered capital requirements include:

- foreign funded printing enterprises whose business scope is printing, packaging and decorative printing materials shall have a registered capital of not less than RMB10 million, while those printing other materials have a lower limit of RMB5 million
- that for a foreign invested holding company in China shall be not less than US$30 million.

In addition, your registered capital is also your limited liability status. So the higher it is, the more credit worthy you are.

However, remember, if the government specifies a minimum "X", and you think you need "Y", and "Y" is bigger, put in "Y"—or ensure you have "Y" from a combination of registered capital and debt financing.

The amount of registered capital needed in the business depends on a number of different factors, some regulatory and some operational:

- *Location (regulatory)*—some regions in China apply different levels of capital requirements than others to reflect their lower or higher regional operational costs.
- *Business scope (regulatory)*—for certain industries or services, the applicable registered capital amount can be quite high. This is sometimes used as a protectionist tool to discourage foreign investment, or to ensure only the right standard of international business can enter the market to guarantee quality of applicant—banking for example has a minimum of US$1 billion. Please note that if some existing businesses wish to expand their current scope of business, it may be a requirement to increase the amount of registered capital.
- *Cashflow (operational)*—this is critical and often overlooked. Registered capital is also required to fund the business operations until it is in a position to fund itself. This should be catered for in the Feasibility Study Report. However, in the rush to attract new investments, and as a result of a lack of even basic economics, many government agents do not pay much attention to detail in this report. Often the happy foreign investor will naively assume he is got a great deal with a "minimum amount" being identified. However, the business can come to a shuddering halt if the registered capital amount is insufficient to support operational cash flow.

Correcting this is not just a simple matter of wiring additional funds to China. Procedures have to be followed since any money sent to make up an operational shortfall that does not follow the government's business cash injection protocol is assumed to be taxable income and can be subject to the 25 percent corporate income tax:

- application to increase the registered capital with the original examining and approving authority, then re-issuing of the Approval Certificate
- application to the State Administration of Foreign Exchange to transfer funds into China
- contribution of 20% of the increased capital within a certain time period from issuance of the new Approval Certificate, and subsequently obtaining the Capital Verification Report
- application to modify the business license with the original registering authority, then re-issuing of business license reflecting this—this is important as the registered capital amount is also the limited liability status of the business
- post-registration procedures of all related certificates such as state and local tax, financial registration, corporate code, etc.

The above steps take between 6 and 10 weeks to implement. If you have already run out of operational money, you by now have not paid staff for 2 months, your suppliers, and possibly your utilities. In effect, your business has been throttled before it even had a chance to breathe.

Registered Capital: The Mechanics

Registered capital can be contributed in cash or in kind, the latter normally being imported equipment or perhaps intellectual property rights (although in kind contributions cannot exceed 70% of the registered capital). Note that it can be time-consuming to inject equipment as registered capital, rather than buying it using the registered capital cash. Locally obtained RMB cannot be injected as registered capital—it must be sent in from the overseas investor.

Reclaiming Registered Capital

After the registered capital is wired into the registered capital account in China, this amount cannot be wired out again freely. The money will be used as operational funds. Some advisors may tell you that you do not need actually to wire the money into China, or they can help you wire the registered capital out of China after the capital is verified. This is totally illegal—do not do this.

2 Specific JV Structural Issues

Management

Many companies leave the entire operations up to the Chinese partner to run. This is a crucial mistake. A new business needs all the support it can get. You need to invest in a foreign manager to keep an eye on things, especially during the early stages. Correct systems, accounting and quality control issues all need to be taken care of. You have standards. Ensure these are implemented and operational in your JV. The ideal solution is an expat manager—if not long-term then certainly for the initial development stages. However, the general manager is responsible for the operations of the business. It is wise to make this one of your personnel. Leaving both in the hands of the Chinese partner effectively hands them control of the business.

Capital Investment

When negotiating the amount here do be sure that the Chinese side's investment really is worth that amount of money. Asset and stock valuations to verify these are a prerequisite. This means having proper valuations placed on machinery—the Chinese tend to quote the original purchase price with no depreciation. Buildings often are valued at the price it would cost today to build and do not actually reflect the fact that it may well be a 15 year old shack that cost US$10,000 to put up in 1988. Also, check the Land Use Rights certificate—if he can show these are granted rights, with no administrative or judicial enforcement measures such as sealing-up, seizure or freezing in connection with the asset, then he owns the land. If they are just allocated, he does not and the right to use it should just be the rental value. See also the "Legal and Financial Due Diligence" section.

Royalties

This can be built in as part of your investment. Protect yourselves also—patents and trademarks should be properly registered in China as being your property if you want to retain control over use of these. Technology transfer can be paid in the form of royalties from the JV—ensure contracts are in place and that you understand the legal and tax implications.

Do not just assume "it'll be taken care of". Be smart. Get it looked after. Withholding tax applies to royalty contracts at a rate lower than profits tax in most cities in China, so get those agreements in there—it saves you money.

Profits Repatriation

Make sure this is adequately addressed. The Chinese partner is not so concerned about this, and would not be familiar with the procedures or mechanisms in any event—he never had to do it. You can pull money out of the business in pre-tax expenses. Also ensure you know the mechanisms and have enhanced your ability to repatriate funds as much as possible. As mentioned—do not rely either on the basic draft contract or your Chinese partner to take care of this. They would not know how to do so. It is your problem, not theirs and they would not have any experience in it. Get professional advice—it saves you money.

Future Mergers & Acquisitions

Be sure to build into the contract and articles proper mechanisms outlining exactly the procedures and protocol for changing ownership, buying and selling shares in the company, share valuations and so on. These are not properly covered in basic drafts, and if the time comes you want to consider this you had better have them in place or you may be stuck. Amendments to the articles of association require government approval. Highlighting your intentions later on may result in problems with getting amendments considered to be in your favour approved. Build the mechanisms in from the start.

Exit Strategy

Clearly define what are to be considered unacceptable levels of business (losses in consecutive years, production below targeted levels, etc.) and have these agreed upon and set in the contract and articles. Often they are not and this can lead to problems with getting you out of a JV if the government does not agree with your assessment of what is and is not a viable business. They have different agendas—keeping people employed, collection of tax revenues and so on. Make sure economic performance is properly identified as a clear reason to effect closure if things do not work out as planned.

3 Technology Transfer Agreements

Introduction

What are they? In short: they are legal frameworks for transferring technology, expertise or facilities from one party to another. This could include importing or exporting technology from outside the territory of the People's Republic of China into the territory of the People's Republic of China or it could involve transfers within China.

This process of technology transfer could be simple and straightforward—but usually it is highly complicated. Before using your contract, have a look at it. Is your contract in compliance with China's laws and regulations? Especially if you want to import or export technology, it is worth noting that there are some rules you should take into account.

Technology Transfer Import and Export

Technology Import

In most cases China permits free technology import and export' except where the laws and regulations of the PRC provide otherwise. It is worth noting that as a general rule the state encourages import of advanced and appropriate technology. But there are also technologies that are restricted or prohibited for importation. Letterpress printing technology and technology that reduces viscosity are some examples on the prohibited list. Others like conventional waste water technology and technology for producing gene engineering strains for use in fermentation, are restricted. You will find the official catalogue (in Chinese) at: http://www.mofcom.gov.cn/aarticle/b/c/200711/20071105200619.html

Import of restricted technology. If you want to import restricted technology you should apply for a technology import letter of intent together with the relevant documents at the competent foreign trade department under the State Council. The department will examine and make a decision on approval or disapproval within 30 working days. If it is approved, a letter of intent for licensing the technology import will be issued by the department. After this you may sign a contract for technology import with your overseas partner.

After signing the technology transfer agreement for technology import with your overseas partner, a copy of the technology transfer agreement and relevant documents shall be submitted to the applicable foreign trade department under the State Council to apply for the technology import license. The department will either approve or disapprove the technology import. If it is approved it will issue the technology import license. The license is necessary to get approval from other relevant departments such as SAFE, SAT and customs.

Import of freely importable technology. Technology that is neither restricted nor prohibited is freely importable, but you need to register your technology with the relevant foreign trade department under the State Council before importing by submitting the following documents:

(a) copy of the agreement;
(b) application letter;
(c) supporting documents proofing legal identity.

Within three working days, the department will register the technology agreement and issue the import registration certificate. The registration certificate is necessary to get approval from other relevant departments such as SAFE, SAT and customs.

Technology Export

The state encourages export of advanced and appropriate technology. But there are also technologies that are restricted or prohibited to export. You will find the official catalogue (in Chinese) at: http://www.mofcom.gov.cn/aarticle/b/e/200207/20020700031702.html.

Export of restricted or prohibited technology. You are not allowed to export any prohibited technology. If you want to export restricted technology, apply for a license issued by the relevant foreign trade department under the State Council. Within 30 working days after receiving your complete application, the department will decide whether to approve or disapprove. If it is approved, a letter of intent for licensing the technology export will be issued by the relevant foreign trade department under the State Council. After this you may sign an agreement with your overseas partner.

The following documents shall be submitted to apply for an export license by the relevant foreign trade department under the State Council:

(a) letter of intent;
(b) copy of the agreement;
(c) description of the technology;
(d) supporting documents proofing legal identity.

The department will approve or disapprove the export of the technology, and if approved issue the technology export license.

Export of freely exportable technology. Technology that is neither restricted nor prohibited is freely exportable. You need to register your technology with the relevant foreign trade department under the State Council before exporting by submitting the following documents:

(a) copy of the agreement;
(b) description of the technology;
(c) supporting documents proofing legal identity.

Within three working days the department will register the technology agreement and issue the export registration certificate.

The license is necessary to get approval from other relevant departments such as SAFE, SAT and customs.

If you import or export restricted or prohibited technology, criminal prosecution for criminal liability or imposition of other penalties could be the potential consequences. The product may be confiscated and a fine could be imposed up to three times as high as the income received. Your business license may also be revoked. Do not do it.

4 Legal and Financial Due Diligence

You must conduct comprehensive due diligence on your potential Joint Venture partner. If you fail to do so, your entire China business may be at risk. Some of the basics you can actually do yourself—other investigation may require professional assistance.

Due diligence can also extend to forensic accounting on a partner's books, as well as political risk and other issues, especially if the JV is sizable. However, this is unlikely to worry most SME JVs and may not be necessary for a simple production unit. However, again, take advice.

Some potential partners may interpret such enquiries as intrusive, or infer that you do not believe them. If they are keen to close a deal quickly, they may try to skirt round such issues. This part of the negotiation process therefore needs to be handled with patience and some sensitivity. However, reliable and serious partners will understand your needs, and that of your foreign parent, in order for these issues to be confirmed. Indeed, if they are doing their job properly, they should also require similar disclosure and transparency from you.

The bottom line here is, take your time, know what you are getting into, and if you are uncomfortable, go elsewhere. The China opportunity will be around for a long time. Do not be rushed.

Business License

Details of who is actually who in the Chinese company, and details of their limited liability must be obtained.

Ask for a copy of their business license. It will list (in Chinese) details of the legally responsible person (Legal Representative), the registered address, the amount of registered capital (which is also the limited liability) and the period of the license. This basic information should be checked off against what you know. If there are any discrepancies, ask the reasons why. Sometimes the answer may be quite reasonable—on other occasions it may alert you to potential difficulties.

It is quite common for the actual legally responsible person to not even be the person you are dealing with. License periods may not be consistent with liabilities—such as the case of the 10 year projected JV with a Chinese partner whose license was due to expire in 3 months time! Check this out and make sure you know with whom you are really dealing, and that they can deliver what they say they can.

Capital Verification Report

This is issued by a Chinese independent CPA firm, confirming the fact that the registered capital as identified on the business license was in fact paid up. If the registered capital has not been paid, not only does this mean your partner has not actually capitalized his business, but it also means he has not complied with limited liability requirements. As a consequence he will also be in breach of his own articles of association, which could cause serious problems in the event of a failure or other legal issues.

Land Use Rights

If land is to be injected as part of an asset in a JV, then you need to see Land Use Rights certificates to establish if they own it or not. Land and any buildings injected should also be valued by a third party valuer—these must be China approved Asset Appraisal Offices. Other assets such as equipment and so on can best be valued by your own people, and compared with the Chinese valuation.

These relate to the status of the land on which your Chinese partner has his premises. Does he own it? Two types of land use rights exist:

- *Allocated rights*—these are issued to a venture for a period of years (check the timeframe) but only give the right to use the land. This is fine, but means any buildings that are erected on it will ultimately benefit the landowner, not your company. Additionally, if the agreement over the land is between the Chinese partner and the landlord directly, what happens if your Chinese partner defaults on the rental? You can be thrown off the land. Check this out and ensure you have agreements in place, such as letters of intent from the landlord directly to circumnavigate this eventuality.
- *Granted rights*—again, issued for a period of years, but these give title to the land during this timeframe. If you are here for the long haul, you may want to consider having granted rights, especially if significant investment is taking place on site. Of course it costs more to "buy the land"—but if such rights are issued in your JV name, you may use these to raise loans in China (giving the granted rights as security) and even profit from any sale of the rights later on. If injecting land as part of JV equity your Chinese partner must provide Granted Land Use Rights otherwise the gesture is meaningless.

It is also important to ascertain whether or not your intended Chinese JV partner actually owns the land he is "injecting" as part of his capital—remember that illegal acquisition of land, especially agricultural land, is a problem in many parts of China. Ownership can be checked with the local Ministry of Land and Resources.

Accounts and Tax Issues

Copies of filed accounts can be difficult to extract from your partner. The reason is often that they have been operating two sets of books—one set internally, which shows the true position, and one officially, which provides the "official" position! Obviously this is illegal, but it is extremely common, not least because of the high level of corporate tax. Official accounts may seriously understate profitability and inflate overheads and business costs to reduce tax liabilities. For this reason your China partner may not want to expose these to you—especially if you have already seen his "real" version of events.

If in doubt, ask for a CPA firm to conduct an "Asset Appraisal Report", which will provide a private confirmation of assets and the close-to-true picture. This probably should not be conducted from the partner's usual accountants. At the very least you will have an idea where discrepancies lie and will be able to pursue these irregularities in private, frank talks with your partner without making him feel as if he is in any danger of being under official scrutiny.

If it were purely a business assessment that needs to be made as to the viability of the partner, then to some extent a pragmatic approach to the Chinese party's reporting methodology may be taken, provided this would not impact on your JV at a later stage. If a valuation is carried out, then this becomes a much more complex issue with far more serious implications. You must have professional advice to explain, for example, why company money is kept in a personal account and to be able to reach understandings on why reporting is carried out in a particular manner.

It is also vitally important to ensure that these same practices are not carried over into the new JV, because:

- the SAT places all Foreign Invested Enterprises in China under Category 1, the highest, in tax bureau monitoring and assessments. You cannot afford to have a lack of accounting transparency, no matter what your partner's previous attitude to this was;
- fines—the SAT can levy up to five times the amount of unpaid tax in late payment penalties. Fancy explaining that to your board if your JV gets caught out?

Financial and Secretarial Compliance

It is vital to be, and to remain in, compliance in both accounting and the corporate secretarial aspects of your new JV business. A lack of attention to detail in the paperwork can seriously jeopardize your operations. So let us have a look at good practice in these areas.

Trademarks/Patents

Have they been registered in China? If not—get them done. Was it your agent who registered it or your parent company directly? We have seen agents registering their client's marks as their own IP. Check it is been done and where ownership lies.

Business Licenses

Are they up to date? You should have annual renewals as well as other pertinent licenses and permits—tax registration certificates, export licenses, customs and foreign currency registrations and so on.

Tax Filings

These need to be conducted on a monthly basis, and audits annually. If you are not conducting such filings you are not in compliance. Keeping the foreign investor deliberately out of compliance in order to have leverage later in case of dispute (or more likely as a bargaining chip if something naughty is being planned) is fairly common. Outsource this or get in at least quarterly checks to ensure all is in place and where it should be.

Reporting also should be to a professional standard and maintained. An inability to provide accounts, audited accounts or on-going documentation is a sign that all is not well. Ensure your reporting and checking systems are in place to prevent this sort of occurrence, and if necessary hire a firm to provide the impartial monitoring you need.

Problems?

These usually show up if your local partner is late in filings, reporting, or is reluctant or unable to fully explain the financial or documentary aspects of the office or business. Resistance to "getting in accountants" is also symptomatic. Accounting is not rocket science at this level, and it is either being handled properly or it is not. It is your responsibility to ensure any problems are resolved.

Outsourcing, or getting in someone qualified, can help resolve the issue of a lack of training and incompetence. Fraud and non-compliance are far more serious and need to be dealt with promptly. Usually a 1 or 2 day site visit by an experienced external accountant is enough to identify whether there are actually problems and the likely extent of these. From there an action plan can be formulated, the issues explored and corrected and the business put back on a compliant platform.

The Memorandum of Understanding (MOU)

When negotiating, it is common practice in China for the Chinese side to introduce the concept of the "Memorandum of Understanding" (MOU).

While not in itself a legally binding document, it is designed to clarify the position of each party and ensure a documented mutual understanding of each other's position. However, many foreign investors do not pay attention to the drafting of this. This is a mistake. The Chinese side will refer back to any items identified within an MOU and if there is any change in a documented agreement, will want to know why. This can lead to a breakdown of communications or mutual trust and hold the negotiation procedures up. Accordingly it is important that attention to detail is paid to the content within the MOU and that anything that may be misconstrued, or that is not intended, be taken out. They act as a basic draft for the JV contract and articles. Getting the MOU wrong from the start and in subsequent drafts can cause tactical negotiation problems later. Pay attention to it.

5 JV Contracts and Articles of Association

AJV can be thought of as having both a "heart" and a "mind". Its "heart" lies in the contract, which specifies the agreement between, and duties of, each party, while the "mind" lies in the Articles of Association, which determines how this is to be accomplished. They are equally vital parts and attention to detail is essential.

Both the JV Contract and Articles of Association are legally binding documents, meaning you may resort to the contract to assert a right or claim damages against your partner, or your partner may make a claim against you. However, the legal binding effect of the JV Contract and Articles of Association is only between the partners who enter into this agreement, and the documents cannot serve as a defence against any third party or government authority. That is to say, if the agreement vested the compliance issue to one party in the JV, and non-compliance is detected later, both parties shall be jointly held legally liable. Nevertheless, it is arguable that the party who is specifically vested with the responsibility for compliance issues should be held solely liable.

Contractual JVs vs Equity JVs

There are two types of JVs in China, the Equity JV (EJV) and the Co-operative JV (CJV) (sometimes known as the Contractual JV). They may appear similar on the surface but have different implications for the structuring of your entity in China. Here we explore the differences, provide practical advice on structuring, tips on investment clawbacks, land use rights and profit distribution.

An EJV is a joint venture between Chinese and foreign partners where the profits and losses are distributed between the parties in proportion to their respective equity interests in the EJV, but the foreign partner shall hold more than 25% of the equity interest in the registered capital of the EJV. The company enjoys limited liability as a "Chinese legal person".

The CJV is a very flexible FIE where Chinese and foreign investors have more contractual freedom to structure cooperation. It is a joint venture between Chinese and foreign investors where the profits and losses are distributed between the parties in accordance with the specific provisions in the CJV contract, not necessarily in proportion to their respective equity interests in the CJV.

In the past, CJVs took one of two different forms—a "true" CJV which did not involve the creation of a legal person that was separate and distinct from the contracting parties; and a "legal person" CJV in which a separate business entity was established and the parties' liability was generally limited to their capital contributions.

In the case of a "true" CJV, each party was responsible for making its own contributions to the venture, paying its own taxes on profit derived from the venture and bearing its own liability for risks and losses. In contrast, a "legal person" CJV, the more prevalent form today, shares more of the characteristics of an EJV. The "true" CJV is rare today as few investors are willing to entertain the prospect of unlimited liability and the rest of this discussion only refers to "legal person" CJVs.

In practice EJVs are more common—10,223 s EJVs were created in 2006, compared to only 1,036 CJVs—although the latter are still used in some specialized fields such as oil exploration.

There are significant operational differences between the contracts and laws governing the two types. The key differences and practical issues are discussed below, and summarized in the table.

- Liability status—EJVs must be established as limited liability companies, while CJVs have the option to operate either as a limited liability company or as a non-legal person. In the latter case, liability is unlimited, but split between the parties in a ratio according to their equity investment. Such entities are run by a "management committee" rather than by a board of directors. They are typically operated in the event of the foreign party making capital contributions to a Chinese manufacturer to upgrade facilities, but then wanting some degree of control as to how that investment is managed.
- Management structure—EJVs must have a two-tier structure, consisting of a board of directors and a contractually appointed management team, usually defined as the "general manager and two deputies" (although the precise number of deputies varies), who have legal responsibility for the daily operations of the business. This is to ensure that the specific management functions of a larger operation are clearly defined. CJVs can operate solely as a board of directors (or management committee if non-legal status), but they must have a general manager as well. For smaller concerns, decision-making responsibility can then rest solely with the board.
- Contractual obligations—in real operational terms, EJVs tend to be far more rigid in their contractual structure, thus lending greater security to the larger amounts of equity that such structures are typically used for, albeit that such security is defined more by state regulations. CJVs allow greater contractual flexibility for the investors to define the obligations of the interested parties.
- Capital contributions—contributions to any JV can be in the form of either cash, or in kind, such as buildings, machinery, materials, and know-how. With EJVs, this process and the value attached to contributions are highly scrutinized. Independent valuers are often used to ensure that "items thus identified are not higher than the prevailing international market prices", as they form an inalienable part of the contractual agreement. CJVs, however, need not have their "investment conditions for co-operation" priced or evaluated, meaning that the JV parties may decide how the value of their contributions should be determined.

- Profit sharing and equity ratios—EJVs are defined contractually as each investor being entitled to profit sharing based upon the proportion of equity owned. Foreign investors may have a minimum of 25% of equity. CJVs differ fundamentally, in that the profit sharing ratio does not have to be tied to the equity stake. Thus, a foreign partner can own less of the equity than the Chinese partner, but take out more in profit. In some restricted industries the foreign partner must own less, such as advertising, telecoms, real estate and transportation. Profits in CJVs can also be taken "in kind", whereby the Chinese party would undertake processing, with the foreign party realizing profits through sale of finished goods. This is common in real estate CJVs, where the Chinese side provides land use rights as their equity, and the foreign side provides the finance, and finished units are then distributed on a contractually agreed ratio as profits.
- Reclaiming capital investment—CJVs, but not EJVs, can theoretically allow for the original capital injected by the foreign party (but not the Chinese) to be recovered in an accelerated repayment structure during the term of the venture. This is of great assistance when the foreign party is using loan capital to finance the venture. The trade off, however, is that the Chinese side then has title to the CJVs assets after the expiration of the JV term.

However, the State Council did issue a Circular in 2002 to deal with such accelerated repayment structures. This now makes it very difficult to obtain approval for such arrangements.

Sample JV Contract and Articles of Association

Here we provide a basic draft of an EJV contract and Articles of Association as commonly used in China for a manufacturing enterprise (CJV versions are generally very similar). As we have discussed, this does need attention to detail and if necessary needs to be redrafted in accordance with your specific situation. Once completed, the contract needs to be translated into Chinese and forms part of the application documentation. It is important that you seek professional advice from a competent firm in China when drafting, as any amendments to them require specific additional government approval—the granting of amendments being not entirely in the investor's own hands.

It should be noted that the JV contract details the responsibilities of each party, while the articles lay down the operating and management rules of the company. As such each are equally important and attention to detail and the implications of both need to be thoroughly understood.

Summary of the differences between EJVs and CJVs

Issue	All JVs	EJVs	CJVs
Liability status		EJVs must be established as limited liability companies	CJVs have the option to operate either as a limited liability company or as a non-legal person
Management structure		EJVs must have a two-tier structure, consisting of a board of directors and a contractually appointed management team, usually defined as the "general manager and two deputies" (precise number of deputies may vary from JV to JV), who have legal responsibility for the daily operations of the business	CJVs can operate solely as a board of directors (or management committee if non-legal status), but they also require a general manager
Contractual obligations		EJVs tend to be far more rigid in their contractual structure	CJVs allow greater contractual flexibility for the investors to define the obligations of the interested parties
Capital contributions		Value attached to contributions are highly scrutinized. Independent valuers are often used	CJVs, need not have their "investment conditions for co-operation" priced or evaluated, meaning that the JV parties may decide how the value of their contributions should be determined
Profit sharing and equity ratios		EJVs are defined contractually as each investor being entitled to profit sharing based upon the proportion of equity owned. Foreign investors may have a minimum of 25% of equity, with no upper limit	CJVs differ fundamentally, in that the profit sharing ratio does not have to be tied to the equity stake

JOINT VENTURE AGREEMENT OF _____ CO., LTD.

Chapter 1

General provisions

In accordance with the *Sino-foreign Equity Joint Venture Law of the People's Republic of China* and other applicable laws and regulations in China, and on the basis of equality and mutual benefit, _____ company, and _____ company have signed a joint venture contract to establish a joint venture enterprise in _____, the People's Republic of China.

5 JV Contracts and Articles of Association

Chapter 2

The parties

Article 1

The parties in the Contract are as follows:
_____ (hereafter Party A)
Registered at: _____, China.
Head office:
Legal representative:
Title:
Nationality: Chinese
_____ (hereafter Party A)
Registered at: _____, [country]
Head office:
Legal representative:
Title:
Nationality:

Chapter 3

Establishment of the joint-venture company

Article 2

In accordance with the *Sino-foreign Equity Joint Venture Law of the People's Republic of China* and other applicable laws and regulations in China, the parties establish a joint venture enterprise, _____, (hereafter the "Enterprise") in China.

Article 3

The Chinese name of the Enterprise is:
The English name of the Enterprise is:
The legal address of the Enterprise:

Article 4

All the business activities of the Enterprise shall be governed by Chinese laws, and other pertinent rules and regulations.

Article 5

The Enterprise shall take the form of be a limited liability company. The parties shall be liable for the Enterprise to the extent of their registered capital contribution.

Chapter 4

Principle and scope of business

Article 6

The parties agree to establish the Enterprise with the purpose of:
[fill in as appropriate]

Article 7

The business scope of the Enterprise is as below:
[fill in as appropriate]

Article 8

Based on the market requirement for its products, services and related technology in both domestic and overseas markets, combined with its own capacity, the expected production scale of the Enterprise will be RMB_____ within ___ years after setup and the annual total sales income will be RMB_____.

Chapter 5

Total amount of investment and registered capital

Article 9

The total amount of investment of the Enterprise is RMB_____.

Article 10

The registered capital of the Enterprise is RMB_____, of which:

(a) Party A contributes RMB_____, accounting for __% of registered capital, comprising [whatever assets are appropriate] (the assets invested by Party A are described in the assets evaluation report confirmed by the parties, details are provided in [relevant attachment] confirmed and signed by the parties).
(b) Party B contributes RMB_____, accounting for __% of registered capital, comprising [whatever assets are appropriate] (the assets invested by Party B are described in assets evaluation report confirmed by the parties, details are provided in [relevant attachment] confirmed and signed by the parties).

Article 11

The parties undertake to contribute their respective capital contributions fully within 3 months from the date of the issuance of the Enterprise's business license.

Article 12

Parties A and B shall assist the Enterprise to obtain possession and land use right of the relevant land (as described in [relevant attachments]) within 3 months from the date of the issuance of the Enterprise's business license. The possession and land use right must be legal and convertible.

Article 13

The procedure of the certificate of land use transference to the Enterprise shall be finished by _____. The Enterprise will be the legal representative on the certificate. All the start-up expenses for the transference shall be paid by Party B, and the relevant tax shall be paid according to the law of China. The term of land use shall be the operation term of the Enterprise. If the land use term needs to be extended, Parties A and B shall assist the Enterprise to apply for extension.

Article 14

After the investment is paid by the parties, a Chinese registered accountant engaged by the Enterprise shall verify it and provide a capital verification report.

Article 15

Any parties wishing to transfer all or some of its investment to a third party must obtain the other parties' approval and submit an approval to the relevant organization. The other party shall have a priority in buying those shares. Any transference of investment in breach of these Articles is totally invalid.

Chapter 6

Obligation of the parties

Article 16

The obligations of Party A are:
1. To assist the Enterprise to apply for approval, registration and business license.
2. To contribute the assets according to Articles 10–12.
3. To assist the Enterprise to purchase or rent equipment, material, office furniture, transportation and communications, etc.
4. To assist the Enterprise to obtain facilities such as water, electricity, environmental protection, etc.
5. To assist the Enterprise to employ local managers, technicians, workers and other staff.

6. To guarantee that it is the owner of the equity invested by it and that they are not subject to any lien, pledge, preemption, subscription right, claim, equity, burden or any other third party's rights. Party A shall be responsible for any damage to the Enterprise that is a result of its breach of the above guarantee and compensate the Enterprise in cash.
7. To guarantee that all the assets invested by it are in line with the current state standards with regard to sanitation, environmental protection, etc. If it is found after the Enterprise has been set up that the assets invested by Party A do not meet the above standards, Party A shall be liable for any additional investment or fine, loss, etc. as a result and compensate the Enterprise in cash.
8. To assist with other relevant tasks authorized by the Enterprise.

The obligations of Party B are:

1. To assist the Enterprise to apply for approval, registration and business license.
2. To obtain the certificate of land use right for the Enterprise according to Article 13.
3. To contribute the assets according to Articles 10–12.
4. To assist the Enterprise to purchase or rent equipment, material, office furniture, transportation and communications, etc.
5. To assist the Enterprise to obtain facilities such as water, electricity, environmental protection, etc.
6. To assist the Enterprise to employ local managers, technicians, workers and other staff.
7. To assist the Enterprise to apply for the visa, working permit and the relevant procedures for foreign staff.
8. To guarantee that it is the owner of the equity invested by it and that they are not subject to any lien, pledge, preemption, subscription right, claim, equity, burden or any other third party's rights. Party B shall be responsible for any damage to the Enterprise that is a result of its breach of the the above guarantee and compensate the Enterprise in cash.
9. To guarantee that all the assets invested by it are in line with the current state standards with regard to sanitation, environmental protection etc. If it is found after the Enterprise has been set up that the assets invested by Party B do not meet the above standards, Party B shall be responsible for any resulting additional investment or fine, loss etc., and compensate the Enterprise in cash.
10. To assist with other relevant tasks authorized by the Enterprise.

5 JV Contracts and Articles of Association

Chapter 7

Products sales

Article 17

The products of the Enterprise will be sold in both domestic and international markets. The initial goals are that the proportion of products sold on the market outside China shall be __-__% of the total products, while the proportion of products sold on the market inside China shall be __-__% of the total products.

Article 18

The exports shall be sold by the Enterprise directly. The products sold inside China will be sold by the Enterprise or the Enterprise may appoint the parties or their subsidiaries to carry out such sales.

Chapter 8

Board of directors

Article 19

The Board of Directors is established from the issuing date of the Enterprise Business License.

Article 20

The Board of Directors shall consist of five (5) directors appointed by the parties. Three members are appointed by Party A, two by Party B. The Chairman shall be appointed by Party A, the deputy-chairman shall be appointed by Party B. The term of office for the Directors is normally 4 years and they may be re-appointed by the parties. The parties may replace any of the Board members at any time by giving advanced notice. Each Board member holds one share of voting power.

Article 21

The Board of Directors shall be the highest authority of the Enterprise. It decides all major issues concerning the Enterprise and supervises all the business activities. Its power and function are as follows:

1. Deciding and approving important reports and plans put forward by the General Manager (e.g. production plan, operation program, investment plan, annual business summary, fund and loans, etc.).
2. Approving annual financial reports, budget, distribution of annual profits.

3. Formulating the major rules and regulations of the Enterprise.
4. Deciding to establish the branches of the Enterprise.
5. Deciding to employ or dismiss the General Manager, Deputy General Manager and other senior management personnel, and their salaries and terms and conditions.
6. Other major issues decided by the board.

A Board meeting must be attended by more than two-thirds of the total number of directors. The following items must be passed by all of the board members:

1. Amending the Articles of Association of the Enterprise.
2. Deciding on the increase and transfer of the registered capital of the Enterprise.
3. Deciding on a merger with other business units or organizations, acquisition of other companies and modification of the structure of the Enterprise.
4. Being in charge of extension termination or expiration of the Enterprise and its liquidation.

Other items shall be passed by a majority of board members.

Article 22

The chairman is the legal representative of the Enterprise. Should the chairman be absent, he should present a proxy in writing

Article 23

The Board of Directors shall convene at least one meeting annually. The board meeting shall be called and presided over by the chairman and held based on a proposal made by more than one third of the total number of directors. The meeting record shall be filed.

Chapter 9

Business management organization

Article 24

A management organization shall be established in the Enterprise, responsible for its business management. The organization shall include a General Manager, and a Deputy General Manager, and other senior staff as appropriate. The General Manager and the Deputy General Manager shall be appointed by the Board of Directors. The Financial Controller, Auditor, and Chief Engineer shall be appointed by Party B. The General Manager shall be present at Board meetings.

Article 25

The General Manager is responsible to the Board of Directors, and is in charge of daily operations of the Enterprise according to the decision of the Board.
The Deputy General Manager shall assist the General Manager in his work and the General Manager shall discuss all major issues with the Deputy General Manager. The Business Management Department may establish several Department Managers who are in charge of the work of each department and carry out the work under instructions of the General Manager.

Article 26

Party A or B may replace any staff appointed by it according to the request of the Board. If the General Manager and the Deputy General Manager are guilty of corruption or serious dereliction of duty, they may be dismissed at any time upon the decision of the Board.

Chapter 10

Supervisor(s)

Article 27

The JV Company will have one supervisor, who shall be jointly appointed by both parties. The term of office of the supervisor shall be 3 years. The supervisor may, after the expiry of his/her term of office, hold a consecutive term upon re-election. The supervisor of the JV Company may exercise the following authorities:

1. Checking the financial situation of the JV Company.
2. Supervising the duty-related acts of the directors and senior managers, and bringing forward proposals on the removal of any director or senior manager who violates any law, administrative regulation, the articles of association or any resolution of the board meetings of the JV Company.
3. Demanding any director or senior manager to make corrections if his/her act has injured the interests of the JV Company.
4. Providing proposals to the board of shareholders.
5. Filing claims against the Board of Directors and senior managers according to related PRC laws.
6. Other duties as prescribed by the articles of association.

Article 28

No director or senior manager of the JV Company may concurrently work as a supervisor of the JV Company.

Article 29

The supervisor shall obey Chapter 6 of the Company Law of the People's Republic of China providing the qualifications and obligations of the directors, supervisors and senior managers of the Company.

Chapter 11

Equipment purchase

Article 30

Materials, fuel, fittings, transportation and office supplies needed by the Enterprise shall be purchased in China where possible. The principle of "high quality while reasonable price" shall be applied to all procurement.

Chapter 12

Labor management

Article 31

The General Manager should be responsible for recruitment, dismissal, labor protection, salary, welfare benefit, and other labor issues for the staff of the Enterprise according to relevant regulations, and report to the Board of Directors for approval. Labor contracts concluded between the Enterprise and its staff shall be filed at local Labor Bureau.

Article 32

The recruitment, salary, welfare benefit, insurance and travel allowances of the senior management personnel shall be decided by the Board. The salary level of senior management personnel may be adjusted based on the profitability and the condition of the Enterprise.

Chapter 13

Tax, finance and accounting

Article 33

The company should pay all taxes required and enjoy tax reduction or tax exemption in accordance with the related regulations of PRC.

5   JV Contracts and Articles of Association 49

Article 34

The staff and workers of the Enterprise should pay individual income tax according to the *Individual Income Tax Law of the PRC*.

Article 35

The Enterprise shall draw reserve funds, developing funds, bonuses and welfare funds for staff and workers from its profit after payment of taxes according to relevant laws. The Board of Directors will decide the proportion of such allocations.

Article 36

The Enterprise shall pay all relevant mandatory welfare benefits for Chinese staff according to the relevant regulations, and show this expense clearly in the cost of the Enterprise.

Article 37

The fiscal year of the Enterprise shall be from January 1 to December 31. All the vouchers, receipts, accounts and reports, forms and quarterly and annual financial reports shall be recorded in Chinese.

Article 38

The financial statement shall be certified and audited by a certified accountant. The result shall be submitted to the Board of Directors and the General Manager.
If any party needs to employ other auditors to audit the financial statement, the other party shall approve it.

Article 39

The General Manager shall prepare a balance sheet, a statement of income and profit distribution proposal in the first 45 days of a fiscal year and submit them to the Board for approval. The audited financial statement shall be submitted to the Board before March 15.

Chapter 14

Duration

Article 40

The duration of the Enterprise shall be 50 years, beginning from the day when the business license is issued.

If proposed by one party and passed by the Board, an application for the extension of duration shall be submitted to the original examination and approval authority 180 days prior to the expiry date.

Chapter 15

Liquidation

Article 41

Upon the termination of the Enterprise or termination before the term expires, the Enterprise shall liquidate the assets according to the law and regulations. After completion of the liquidation, the assets shall be disposed according to the investment proportion contributed by the parties.

Chapter 16

Force majeure

Article 42

If any party cannot fulfill its obligations under this Agreement due to force majeure, including earthquake, strikes, fires, flood, war, or actions that cannot be predicted and avoided, the party shall inform the other by the fastest means possible. The details of the force majeure, the reason and the valid certificate of inability to fulfill the obligations shall be provided within 15 days by the administration of the area in which the force majeure occurs. The termination, deference or the exemption of obligation shall be negotiated and decided by the parties.

Chapter 17

Applicable law

Article 43

The formation of the Agreement, its validity, interpretation, execution and settlement of any disputes arising hereunder shall be governed by and constructed in accordance with the laws and the regulations of the People's Republic of China.

Chapter 18

Dispute resolution

Article 44

In the case of disputes arising over this Agreement or any matters related hereto, the parties shall negotiate in good faith to resolve such disputes. If such negotiation fails, the parties shall submit the dispute to arbitration by _____ in accordance with its arbitration rules. The decision of the arbitrage body is final and shall be binding to the parties hereto.

Article 45

Until the dispute is resolved, the Agreement shall remain valid, except the part that is in dispute.

Chapter 19

Written language

Article 46

The Agreement is written in Chinese. There are _____ originals of the Agreement. Each party keeps two originals, the remainder of the originals are filed with the approval authorities, and copies are filed with relevant departments.

Chapter 20

Other issues

Article 47

The attachments to the Agreement [list these] are an inseparable part of the Agreement and equally enforceable.

Article 48

The Agreement shall be approved by _____ and shall become effective upon the signing thereof by the parties thereto.

Article 49

The Agreement is signed in _____, China by authorized representatives of the Parties on _____.

Party A [stamp and chop]
Legal Representative [sign]
_____, in _____
Party B [stamp and chop]
Legal Representative [sign]
_____, in _____

Sample JV Articles of Association

JOINT VENTURE AGREEMENT OF CO., LTD.
  Contents
  Chapter 1   General provisions
  Chapter 2   Purpose and scope of business
  Chapter 3   The total amount of investment and the registered capital
  Chapter 4   The board of directors
  Chapter 5   Business management organization
  Chapter 6   Finance and accounting
  Chapter 7   Distribution of profits sharing
  Chapter 8   Staff and workers
  Chapter 9   Trade union organization
  Chapter 10   Duration, termination and liquidation
  Chapter 11   Rules and regulations
  Chapter 12   Supplementary articles

Chapter 1

General provisions

Article 1

In accordance with the *Sino-foreign Equity Joint Venture Law of the People's Republic of China* and other applicable laws and regulations, _____ (hereinafter referred to as Parry A), and _____ (hereinafter referred to Party B), signed the contract on _____ in _____ regarding [JV company name], the articles of association hereby are formulated.

Article 2

The Chinese name of the Enterprise is:
The English name of the Enterprise is:
The legal address of the Enterprise:

5 JV Contracts and Articles of Association

Article 3

The name and legal address of investor company are as follows:
_____ (hereafter Party A)
Head office:
_____ (hereafter Party A)
Registered at: _____, [country]
Head office:

Article 4

The company shall be a limited liability company.

Article 5

The company is approved by the Chinese government and registered in China. It has the status of a legal person and is subject to the jurisdiction and protection of relevant laws of the PRC.

Chapter 2

Purpose and scope of business

Article 6

The purpose of the company is to boost the industry development of _____, strengthen economic cooperation and technological communication, adopt advanced and appropriate technology, provide financial support, improve the quality of products, develop new products, and enhance the quality and price to boost the competitive capability in local and international market.

Article 7

The business scope of the company is to [fill in as appropriate].

Article 8

Production scale.
Based on the market requirement for its products, services and related technology in both domestic and overseas markets, combined with its own capacity, the expected production scale of the Enterprise will be RMB_____ within ____ years after setup and the annual total sales income will be RMB_____.

Article 9

The products of the Enterprise will be sold in both domestic and international markets. The initial goals are that the proportion of products sold on the market outside China shall be __-__% of the total products, while the proportion of products sold on the market inside China shall be __-__% of the total products.

Chapter 3

The total amount of investment and registered capital

Article 10

The total amount of investment of the Enterprise is RMB_____.

Article 11

The registered capital of the Enterprise is RMB_____, of which:

(c) Party A contributes RMB_____, accounting for __% of registered capital, comprising [whatever assets are appropriate] (the assets invested by Party A are described in the assets evaluation report confirmed by the parties, details are provided in [relevant attachment] confirmed and signed by the parties).
(d) Party B contributes RMB_____, accounting for __% of registered capital, comprising [whatever assets are appropriate] (the assets invested by Party B are described in assets evaluation report confirmed by the parties, details are provided in [relevant attachment] confirmed and signed by the parties).

Article 12

Parties A and B shall subscribe the investment according to the terms stated in the contract.

Article 13

After the investment is paid by Parties A and B, a Chinese registered accountant engaged by the Enterprise shall verify it and provide a capital verification report, which shall be submitted to the original examination approval authority and the industrial and commercial bureau.

Article 14

Within the term of the business, the company shall not reduce its registered capital.

5 JV Contracts and Articles of Association

Article 15

Any parties wishing to transfer all or some of its investment to a third party must obtain the other parties' approval and submit an approval to the relevant organization. The other party shall have priority in buying those shares. Any transference of investment in breach of this Article is invalid.

Article 16

Any increase or transfer of the registered capital of the company shall be approved by the board of directors and submitted to the original examination approval authority for approval. The registration procedure for changes shall be dealt with at the original registration and administration office.

Chapter 4

Board of Directors

Article 17

The Board of Directors shall be the highest authority of the Enterprise. It decides all major issues concerning the Enterprise and supervises all the business activities. Its power and function are as follows:

1. Deciding and approving important reports and plans put forward by the General Manager (e.g., production plan, operation program, investment plan, annual business summary, fund and loans, etc.).
2. Approving annual financial reports, budget, distribution of annual profits.
3. Formulating the major rules and regulations of the Enterprise.
4. Deciding to establish the branches of the Enterprise.
5. Deciding to employ or dismiss the General Manager, Deputy General Manager and other senior supervisors, and being responsible for their salaries and terms and conditions.
6. Other major issues decided by the Board.

A board meeting must be attended by more than two-thirds of the total number of directors. The following items must be passed by all of the board members:

1. Amending the Articles of Association of the Enterprise.
2. Deciding the increase and transfer of the registered capital of the Enterprise.
3. Deciding a merger with other business units or organizations, acquisition of other companies and modification of the structure of the Enterprise.

4. Being in charge of extension, termination or expiration of the Enterprise and its liquidation.

Other items shall be passed by a majority of board members.

Article 18

The board of Directors shall consist of five (5) directors appointed by the parties. Three members are appointed by Party A, two by Party B. The chairman shall be appointed by Party A, the deputy-chairman is appointed by Party B. The term of office for the directors is normally 4 years and they may be re-appointed by the parties. The parties may replace any of the board members at any time with a further notice. Each board member holds one share of voting power.

Article 19

A written notice shall be submitted to the board when the two parties need to appoint or replace directors.

Article 20

The board of Directors shall convene the board meeting at least once a year. An interim meeting of the board of Directors may be held based on a proposal of more than one third of the total number of directors.

Article 21

The board meeting should be held at the registered location of the company or other place if appropriate and agreed upon.

Article 22

The board meeting shall be called and presided over by the chairman. Should the chairman be absent, the deputy-chairman shall call and preside over the meeting.

Article 23

The chairman shall give each director a written notice 30 days before the date of the board meeting. The notice shall cover the agenda, time and place of the meeting.

Article 24

Should the chairman be unable to attend the board meeting, he may present a written proxy to the board. In case the chairman neither attends nor entrusts others to attend the meeting, he will be regarded as having abstained.

Article 25

The valid number of participants of the board meeting shall be above two-thirds of the total number of directors.

Article 26

Should the board meeting be postponed because the valid number of participants cannot be met, the chairman shall again give each director a written notice 30 days before the date of the board meeting. The valid number of participants for the new board meeting shall be automatically changed to half of the total number of the directors.

Article 27

A detailed written record shall be kept of every board meeting, which every director should sign and keep one copy.

Chapter 5

The Supervisor

Article 28

Enterprises established after January 1, 2006, shall have at least one Supervisor appointed by a meeting of the shareholders for a 3-year, (renewable) term of office. The Enterprise's directors and senior management personnel shall not concurrently hold the position of Supervisor.
The Supervisor (like the company directors) is not required to reside in or visit the PRC.

Article 29

The Supervisor shall have the following responsibilities:
- checking the financial affairs of the company
- supervising the duty-related acts of the directors and senior management personnel, and in the case that any violation of law, administrative regulation, Articles of Association or any resolution of the shareholders meeting has taken place, proposing their removal from the company
- demanding that any director or senior management personnel make rectifications if his act has injured the interests of the company
- attending the Board of Directors meetings and raising questions or suggestions on the matters to be decided by the Board of Directors

- making investigations for the company—if the company is found to be running abnormally, and should it be deemed necessary, the Supervisor may engage an accounting firm to assist in the ensuing investigations
- other responsibilities provided for by Company Law and the Articles of Association.

Article 30

The expenses necessary for the Supervisor to perform his duties shall be borne by the company.

Chapter 6

Business management organization

Article 31

A management organization shall be established in the company, which is responsible for daily business management.

Article 32

The company shall have one General Manager and one Deputy General Manager. The General Manager and Deputy General Manager shall be appointed by the Board of the Directors.

Article 33

The General Manager is in charge of the daily operations of the company according to the Articles of Association and the Board Resolutions, as well as organizing and managing the daily production, technology and management. The Deputy General Manager shall assist the General Manager in his work.

The powers of the General Manager are as follows:
1. To organize and conduct the daily production, technology and operation and management of the company, and carry out the resolution of the Board of Directors.
2. To organize and conduct the annual operating plan and investment plan of the company.
3. To formulate the internal management of the company.
4. To detail the policy of the JV company.
5. To handle staff recruitment and HR.

Article 34

When deciding on important issues, both the General Manager and the Deputy General Manager shall sign relevant documents and contracts.

Article 35

The term of office for the General Manager and the Deputy General Manager may be renewed at the invitation of the Board of Directors.

Article 36

The General Manager or Deputy General Manager shall not have any involvement with any organization that is in competition with the company.
The General Manager or Deputy General Manager shall not have any involvement with any organization that is in competition with the company.

Article 37

The company shall have one Financial Controller and Auditor assigned by Party B The financial controller shall exercise leadership in the financial and accounting affairs of the company.

Article 38

The auditor shall be in charge of the auditing work of the company, examine and check the financial receipts, expenditure and the accounts, and submit written reports to the General Manager and the Board of Directors.

Article 39

The General Manager, Deputy General Manager, Chief Engineer, Financial Controller, Auditor and other senior management personnel who wish to resign shall do so in writing to the Board of Directors and shall give 3 months notice.
If the General Manager, Deputy General Manager or other senior management is guilty of corruption or serious dereliction of duty, they may be dismissed at any time upon the decision of the board.

Chapter 7

Finance and accounting

Article 40

The finance and accounting of the JV company shall be handled in accordance with Chinese laws and the applicable regulations of the Ministry of Finance of the

PRC and the situation of the company. Such issues will also be calculated and managed according to the related financial accounting standards of the foreign invested company.

Article 41

The fiscal year of the company shall be from January 1 to December 31.

Article 42

All vouchers, account books, statistical statements and reports of the company shall be written in Chinese.

Article 43

The company adopts Renminbi (RMB) for its accounts. The conversion of the RMB into other currency shall be in accordance with the exchange rate of the converting day published by the State Administration of Foreign Exchange.

Article 44

The company shall open accounts in RMB and foreign currency with the Bank of China or other banks agreed by the Chinese government.

Article 45

The company shall adopt internationally used accrual basis and both debit and credit accounts for its bookkeeping.

Article 46

The following items shall be covered in the financial account books:

1. The amount of overall cash receipts and expense of the company.
2. All material purchased and sold by the company.
3. The registered capital and debts of the company.
4. The time of payment, increase and transfer of the registered capital of the company.

Article 47

The finance department of the JV company shall work out the statement of assets and liability and losses and gains accounts of the past year in the first 45 days of each fiscal year, and submit this information via the General Manager to the board of the meeting for approval after being examined and signed by the auditor.

Article 48

Parties A and B have the right to inspect the financial account books using their own auditor.

Article 49

The company shall decide on the term of depreciation of fixed assets and amortization of intangible assets according to relevant regulations and standards.

Article 50

All matters concerning foreign exchange shall be handled in accordance with the *Provisional Regulations for Exchange Control of PRC*, and other relevant regulations.

Article 51

The General Manager shall prepare a balance sheet, a statement of income and profit distribution proposal in the first 45 days of a fiscal year and submit them to the board for approval. The financial statement, after auditing, shall be submitted to the board before March 15.

Article 52

The half year accounting report shall be handed to the Board of Directors for inspection before August 1 every year. The monthly accounting report shall be submitted to the investment parties before the middle of the following month.

Article 53

The company shall set up an internal auditing department, led by the auditor and working independently, reporting to the General Manager and reporting directly to the Board of Directors if necessary.

Chapter 8

Distribution of profits sharing

Article 54

The profit of the company should be adjusted in accordance with national regulations. The staff and workers of the company should pay individual income tax according to the *Individual Income Tax Law of PRC*.

Article 55

The company shall allocate reserve funds, expansion funds and bonuses and welfare funds for staff and workers after payment of income taxes. The proportion of allocation is decided by the Board of Directors in accordance with national regulations.

Article 56

After paying income tax in accordance with law and allocating the various funds, the remaining profits shall be distributed in RMB in accordance with the company contract. The company shall help Party B to remit profit abroad according to relevant regulations concerning foreign currency.

Article 57

The General Manager shall declare the profit distribution plan and the amount of the profit the investment parties may receive within 45 days after each fiscal year, then submit it to the Board Meeting for approval. The General Manager may formulate the additional profit distribution plan and the amount of each party based on the actual situation every fiscal year, then submit it to the Board Meeting for approval.

Article 58

The company shall distribute profits only once a year to the investor companies.

Article 59

The company shall not distribute profits unless the losses of previous fiscal year have been made up. Remaining profit from the previous year can be distributed together with that of the current year.

Chapter 9

Staff and workers

Article 60

The company shall employ staff and workers through public recruitment and sign appropriate contracts. Labor contracts concluded between the Enterprise and its staff shall be filed at the local Labor Bureau.

Article 61

The company has the right to take appropriate disciplinary action against those staff and workers who violate the rules and regulations of the company. Serious cases may be dismissed in accordance with relevant regulations.

Article 62

Salary levels shall be decided by the board according to relevant regulations and the actual situation of the company, and specified in detail in labor contracts. Such levels may be adjusted from time to time based on the development of the company's production, business capability and technology level of the staff.

Article 63

Rules relating to welfare benefits, labor insurance, labor protection and labor discipline shall be stated in the company regulations..

Chapter 10

Trade union organization

Article 64

The staff and workers of the company have the right to establish a trade union organization and carry out activities in accordance with the stipulations of the *Trade Union Law of the People's Republic of China.*

Article 65

The Trade Union is representative of the interests of the staff and workers. The tasks of the trade union are:

1. To protect the democratic rights and material interests of the staff and workers pursuant to the law.
2. To strive to fulfill the economic tasks of the company.
3. To assist the company to arrange and make rational use of welfare funds and bonuses.
4. To organize political, professional, scientific and technical studies, and literary, art and sports activities.
5. To educate staff and workers to observe labor discipline.

Article 66

The persons in charge of the Trade Union have the right to attend the board meetings during discussions about the development plan, production management and other important issues of the company, in order to reflect the opinions and requirements of the employees.

Article 67

The Trade Union shall help to solve any dispute between the staff and the company.

Article 68

The company shall allot an amount totaling 2% of all the salaries of the staff and workers as trade union funds, which shall be used by the trade union in accordance with the *Managerial Rules for the Trade Union Funds* formulated by the All China Federation of Trade Unions.

Chapter 11

Duration, termination and liquidation

Article 69

The duration of the company shall be 50 years, calculated from the day when business license is issued.

Article 70

An application for the extension of duration shall be submitted to the original examination and approval authority 180 days prior to the expiry date if Parties A and B agree to extend the duration of the JV company.

Article 71

The Board of Directors shall have the right to terminate the company before the expiry of the term, if the two parties agree it is in the best interests of shareholders. Termination of the company before the term expires shall be decided by the Board of Directors, and shall be submitted to the original examination and approval authority for approval.

Article 72

Either Party A or B shall have the right to terminate the company in case one of the following situations occurs:
 1. If either Party fails to implement their responsibilities as specified in the contract or Articles of Association, or seriously violates the regulation in the contract or the Articles of Association.
 2. The company fails to implement its responsibilities because of force majeure.

Article 73

Upon the termination of the company the Board of Directors shall set up a Liquidation Committee and liquidate the company's assets according to the law.

Article 74

The Liquidation Committee shall assess overall assets, liabilities and equity of the company, and prepare a detailed asset and liability report, and asset listing with the value and base of evaluation and liquidation plan and report to the board for approval.

Article 75

During the liquidation, the Liquidation Committee should go to court and defend on behalf of the company.

Article 76

The expenditure and salary of the Liquidation Committee are paid out of the residual assets of the company as first priority.

Article 77

The remaining property, after the clearance of debts of the company, shall be distributed to the parties according to the percentage of registered capital invested.

Article 78

On completion of the liquidation, the company shall submit a liquidation report to the original examination and approval authority, go through the formalities for cancelling its registration in the original registration office and hand in its business license, and at the same time, make a public announcement.

Article 79

The accounting vouchers, account books and documents shall be handed to Party A for retention.

Chapter 12

Rules and regulations

Article 80

The following rules and regulations can be formulated by the Board of Directors:

1. Management regulations, including the powers and functions of the managerial departments and their working rules and procedures.
2. Rules for the staff and workers.
3. System of labor and salary.

4. System of work attendance record, promotion and awards and penalty for the staff and workers.
5. System of staff and worker's welfare.
6. Financial system.
7. Liquidation procedures.
8. Other necessary rules and regulations.

Chapter 13

Supplementary articles

Article 81

Any amendment to the Articles of Association shall be unanimously agreed and decided by the Board of Directors and submitted to the original examination and approval authority for approval.

Article 82

These Articles of Association, and any amendments shall come into effect upon the approval by the Ministry of Commerce.

Article 83

These Articles of Association are signed in _____, China by authorized representatives of the Parties on _____.
Party A [seal]
Legal Representative [sign]
_____, in _____
Party B [seal]
Legal Representative [sign]
_____, in _____

6 The Application Process

The application process to create a JV can be divided into two parts:
- pre-registration—what happens before the JV formally exists;
- post-registration—what happens after the JV formally exists.

This is done at provincial or municipal level (e.g., Guangdong Province, Shanghai Municipality, Beijing Municipality, etc.), albeit with input from local offices of state-level authorities. In addition, the five Special Economic Zones in South China have independent approval authority over this issue.

We now explain this in more detail.

Pre-registration

Name Pre-approval

The relevant authority is the State Administration for Industry and Commerce (SAIC). This bureau administers the registration of all kinds of enterprises (including FIEs), organizations or individuals that are engaged in business activities; examines and ratifies the registration of business names; and reviews, approves and issues business licenses. Verification of feasibility of the proposed name by SAIC will take a few working days.

Only the Chinese name will be legally binding—the English name is not legally relevant for Chinese authorities. The word "China" cannot be freely included in the Chinese name. The name can be translated by meaning and/or phonetically.

Environmental Impact Report

This is intended to control manufacturing production processes according to specified environmental norms. The Environmental Protection Bureau will require information about the raw materials used, the machinery and equipment, consumption and safe disposal of toxic products. In some cases, a full report on the environmental impact issued by an appointed agent shall be required (for example in the chemical or leather processing business) and this may represent a major step to go through as it would affect the time-frame required to get your factory up and running.

Issue of Approval Certificate and Business License

The authorities will issue the Approval Certificate and Business License after assessing the following documentation:
   From the investor

- business license (certificate of incorporation—please note that depending upon location, this may need to be notarized in the investor's country of origin, then translated into Chinese by a registered translation company)
- bank statement to demonstrate credit worthiness (from relevant bank in country of origin then translated into Chinese)
- photocopy of passport of the Legal Representative of the investor company
- for foreign-funded commercial enterprises, the audit report of the recent fiscal year.

From the new JV

- *about the new business*—name of the company, business scope, registered capital, business term, lease contract
- *about the Legal Representative*—photocopy of passport and passport size photos
- *about the directors*—CVs, photocopy of passport and passport size photos
- Feasibility Study Report
- Articles of Association
- Environmental Impact Report.

The Certificate of Approval will be issued by the local office of the Ministry of Commerce (MOFCOM). After the MOFCOM issues the Certificate of Approval, there is a 30 day limit for the registration of the JV with SAIC, who then issues the Business License.

After that step the WFOE now legally exists.

Post-registration

However, the paperwork does not stop there! You still have quite a bit to do before you have a fully functioning JV. This consists of:

1. Enterprise Code Registration with the Technical Supervision Bureau.
2. Obtaining chops from Public Security Bureau.
3. Office inspection by the Tax Bureau and tax registration.
4. Registration with the State Administration of Foreign Exchange.
5. Opening RMB and foreign currency bank account (if needed).
6. Opening Capital bank account.
7. Customs registration.
8. Financial registration.
9. Statistics registration.
10. Commodity inspection with Commodity Inspection Bureau.
11. Injection of capital and Capital Verification Report.
12. Renewal of business license by SAIC after capital has been injected.
13. Application for General Tax Payer status.

Please note many consultants and law firms do not regard post-registration procedures as part of their scope of work when processing client's applications—so either shop around for a firm that does, or ensure you have this vital component catered for elsewhere. Not following through correctly on these procedures can lead you to non-compliance and government penalties later on.

Other Pre- and Post-registration Issues to Consider

Corporate Name Translations

It is important to spend time to obtain an appropriate translation of the company name, and to try to use it as a uniform translation, when applying for business registration, applying for trademark registrations and so on. It is your corporate identity in China. A uniform Chinese name will be good for marketing and will also avoid later troubles with on-going documentation and application procedures.

Under-estimating Additional Licensing Requirements

Certain JVs have other specific licenses that they may need to obtain in order to operate. These can often be far more difficult to process and obtain than the original license! For example, import and sale of consumable products, trading of certain metals, rare earths, fuel, and pharmaceuticals all require additional licensing applications and need a full understanding of the processing of these in order for you to dovetail all regulatory demands into your business operations in a timely manner.

7 Intellectual Property

Intellectual property has always been a big concern for foreign investors in China. Since the enforcement of IP laws is not so satisfactory at present, it is very important for foreign investors to know how to protect their intellectual property before any infringement occurs. In a JV, of course, you may well be bringing important IP into the business as a resource, and will need to be especially careful to protect it—and remember that it is not just your asset, but it becomes a shared asset with your partner. He should be as interested in protecting it as you are.

Is It Worth It?

IP is an emotive issue to foreign businesses in China. But it is also important to assess the actual damage against the cost of litigation and emotions. Lawyers are expensive, and emotions can mean you concentrate more on the litigation than the case actually warrants. It is wise not to overstate the damage caused to your firm if you do get ripped off and be somewhat pragmatic about dealing with it.

Is Your IP Vital to Your China or International Business?

If it is, you may need seriously to assess whether or not you wish to introduce your technology at all to the market here—this may be part of your initial judgement about whether a JV is indeed appropriate. Or assess the amount of time you have with your IP as part of your marketing plan, to work out how long you are likely to have a free range before the plagiarists get to work and start to erode the market share.

IP in the Legal System and Enforcement

Despite some comment to the contrary, China's courts are improving in upholding claims of plagiarism. It is also worth noting that the vast majority of infringements in China are between Chinese firms themselves, and it is not only international firms that are being targeted. Most of the valuable brands in China are of course Chinese—mass sales of foreign products in China is still fairly limited. Courts can and do, in the main, uphold claims by foreign companies where the evidence is properly introduced and in order. The problem is not with the judiciary, although they are not perfect either. The main issue is that of enforcement—actually stopping the infringement once a judgment in your favor has been awarded.

Trademarks and Patents

You may believe that because you have already registered your trademark elsewhere, it is covered automatically in China. China is signatory to all the international protocols that the international community has drawn up concerning the registration and protection of international IP. Therefore, China follows the same system as most nations follow.

This includes registration of your mark. If your mark has been registered under the Madrid Protocol, you can apply for extended protection in China. After examination by the Trademark Office of China, you may get a Registration Certificate of the Trademark, but this is not necessarily the result. Sometimes your application for extended protection may be rejected on grounds such as similarity with other registered trademarks in the same sub-class, and the process for review shall take at least 2 years. International recognition is only granted provided your mark has previously been registered in five other jurisdictions (thus proving its "international" status) or can be otherwise argued as an "internationally recognized brand"—which is a debatable point and subject to legal interpretation. This means if you have only registered your mark in your home country, you are not covered in China. For practical purposes however, even if you have international protection, we still recommend registering in China as courts may have difficulty in recognizing international protocols if they are not used to them, and this will mean more time and expense in legal fees to educate the court and provide evidence of the significance of such protocols and China's adherence to them. Trademark registration in any event is inexpensive and should be undertaken as a matter of good business sense.

Patent infringement is becoming more and more common, and combating this is a major challenge for foreign companies. When you come to China, you need to consider how to ensure your competitors will not pirate your key technologies. Patent application will be the first step. Careful drafting of the application will help your patent to be approved by the patent authority without too many changes, so you can enjoy the broadest protection allowed by law. In many patent lawsuits, the patentee loses the case simply because of the bad wording of the claims. Therefore, it is very important to find a professional, reliable firm to take care of your patent application.

Patents are further classified into inventions, utilities models and designs under Chinese Patent Law. The official fees for patent application will vary depending on the specific application and the category, for both the initial registration and renewal. Invention patents are for 20 years, and a utility model or design for 10 years. Unlike trademarks, once the period of validity of a patent expires, it cannot be renewed.

As mentioned, China is signatory to various international protocols when it comes to registrations of patents and trademarks. There is, however, a hole in the registration procedure for patents, which require they be registered and placed on public file for assessment prior to the patent being recognized as your own intellectual property. This means some entrepreneurial types scan such registrations specifically to steal designs and then immediately get into production even while your patent pending process is still on-going. This is not a China issue—it is a weakness in the international protocol of registrations and needs to be addressed in the fullest sense to protect expensive R&D and inventions from being used on the cheap by less scrupulous businesses.

Domain Names

With the rapid expansion of the Internet, more and more people have realized the importance of domain names. Usually, a company will register its trademark or its enterprise name as their domain name, and a good domain name ending ".cn" will be very useful for marketing. Domain name registration follows the principle of "first come, first served". It is very important to register the trademark/enterprise name before it is hijacked by others. A simple search of your company name or trademark on the Internet will show the importance of a domain name. The annual fees for registering such a domain name are very low.

Trade Secrets

"Trade secrets" is a very broad concept, and it may include all the information and documents that will bring economic benefits to the company and that should be protected by the company—this will include client information, price, design, production methods and procedures, programs, etc. Trade secrets should not only be protected from competitors, but also amongst key personnel of the company.

Once your company is in the position of negotiation (e.g. for joint venture setup or an OEM contract) with another party and you need to disclose some of your trade secrets, be sure to sign a confidentiality agreement with the other parties and clearly show them what you are sharing as trade secrets.

For key personnel in charge of your trade secrets, a confidentiality agreement and sometimes also a non-competition agreement are also recommended. However, since non-competition agreements also fall within the scope of labor law, it is very important for the company to make sure that all the clauses in the non-competition agreement are in compliance with employment laws.

IP Management System

Intellectual property protection is very professional and complicated work. We suggest your company should have a person in charge of its IP related matters, building and keeping files, coordinating with external IP counsels, monitoring of the IP status, etc.

It will also be helpful to educate your employees to improve their IP consciousness, especially the sales people who are most familiar with the market and the distribution of fake products. Good communication with your clients will also help you to find clues on infringement.

Specific JV IP Issues

Protecting IP

If the foreign investor does not wish to share their IP with the local partner, he should register its IP in China immediately, and let the JV use the IP under license only.

The alternative is to register the IP as "mutual IP", specifying who is to become the owner when co-operation is terminated, as well as the owner of the developed IP during the JV co-operation.

Using IP as Capital Contribution to a JV

Many foreign investors ask whether they can use IP as a capital contribution to a JV instead of contributing cash. Often it is not favourable to do so. IP used in this way has to be already patented in China or a trademark registered in China, and they must be transferred to the contemplated JV. If this happens, then your parent company would have to be licensed by the JV to use what was formerly its own property. It is better to license the IP to the JV and receive a royalty.

Development Zones

An important part of your business plan is clearly answering the question of exactly where in China you will set it up. China is a huge country, and if you have flexibility it is almost always worth considering several options. Costs, infrastructure and markets vary widely from north to south, east to west, as various regions of the country are at differing stages of development.

Of course in some cases you may be forced to go to a particular location, for example if you are following a partner company into China or have very specific business needs. But for the purposes of this discussion we will assume you want to explore several alternative places.

Like most developing countries, China still offers a number of advantages for foreign investors. These can be quite significant and you need to understand what is available that may suit your business plans.

Since the early 1980s, following the opening up of the Chinese economy, development zones began appearing in China. Their success largely stems from the preferential policies they offer and the safe investment environment they create. They do tend to share advantages such as convenient locations, modern developed infrastructure, rich human resources and efficient management and services.

Often the name differences refer to duty levels and import/export restrictions. But the differences can be, by far, greater than the similarities. For manufacturing investors in China, choosing a development zone as their base is the first step in an enormous risk-hedging exercise. Most consider at least three, or as many as five. As every zone has a personality of its own, it is essential to look beyond the pamphlets and the published information, and get down to the details.

The key points to consider, however, will still be whether the added value brought by location, local administration and services, will justify an operation in dearer development zones. Quality and supply of infrastructure, labor availability, proximity to local suppliers and major transport infrastructures are also major issues to be considered prior to any commitment. Also remember that land purchase costs and premises rents are negotiable even within the same zone, and it is thus advisable to shop around to find a suitable location before deciding to invest in a special zone. Infrastructure charges vary too.

Readers should be aware that the Ministry of Land and Resources and other government departments concluded an unprecedented nationwide probe into rampant land abuses in development zones in 2003. The investigation has resulted in the shutting-down of 4,735 development zones, about 70 per cent of the nation's total, and some policy restraint on expansion remains in place. Most problems arose at the level of provincial zones.

Investors should ensure, particularly with provincial and municipal level zones, that the zone authorities have appropriate central government permission for all the incentives that they offer.

In addition, China's accession to the WTO may lead to a changing role for such zones, as distinctions between incentives for foreign and domestic firms and tariffs and non-tariff barriers begin to disappear. However, they are unlikely to disappear completely; most of the zones are well located geographically for international trade and can offer a level of service to investors above that of non-zone areas, and many are beginning to specialize in particular industries.

China currently has just over 2,000 development zones, covering around 13,700 sq. km of land. The main types of state-level zone are described below. In addition, there are also many municipal and provincial level zones, amongst other types.

Readers should be aware that the titles of many Chinese zones can be expressed in several different ways in English, adding confusion as to which is which and what type they are.

See the website of the China Association of Development Zones (http://www.cadz.org.cn/en/) for more details of the major state-level zones.

The main state-level types and their characteristics are as follows:

Special Economic Zones (SEZs)

- first type of Chinese DZ, dating from early 1980s; all in South China in Shenzhen, Shantou, Xiamen, Zhuhai, and Haikou
- aimed at a wide spectrum of industry
- the five cities retain rights to enact their own relevant legislation without reference to their provincial government
- closed areas for which nationals from other regions may require a special permit to visit.

Economic and Technological Development Zones (ETDZs)

- 90 nationwide—every province, municipality and autonomous region has at least one, coastal areas have several each—the earliest date from 1982 to 1984, later spread inland

- tend to be aimed at technology-intensive industries and to focus on several key sectors each
- many now include Export Processing Zones (see below)
- Hi-Tech companies and SMEs may still attract a 15% rate, otherwise the unified rate of 25% applies from 2008.

High-Tech Industrial Development Zones (HIDZs)

- 67 nationwide, every province has at least one (except Tibet, Ningxia, Qinghai)—they date from 1990s
- sometimes known as New and High-Technology DZs, High Tech Parks or New Districts
- they are aimed primarily at commercializing the results of scientific research, and thus encourage industries such as IT, electronics, pharmaceuticals, new materials, etc.—they are all part of the "Torch" program of scientific development and are often located next to universities. Again, the 15% rate may apply for some hi-tech applications, otherwise the new 25% rate kicks in from 2008.

Free Trade Zones (FTZs)

- 15 in total, all coastal obviously, next to ports, usually about 6–10 km^2, dating from 1990s
- "inside the territory, outside the Customs"—specialized areas for international trade and bonded operations within the area, with warehousing, bonded areas and logistics facilities
- various VAT, tax and other incentives
- many companies who are manufacturing for export are located in these zones.

Export Processing Zones (EPZs)

- 60 in all, many coastal, but many newer ones inland
- fairly new type of DZ—created since 2000, all around 2–3 km^2 or less, generally within an existing DZ, usually ETDZ
- simpler mechanism than FTZs for export processing. Incentives are given to High-Tech applications.

Human Resources

This section explains some other general HR issues that you will need to take into account when establishing your JV. Please also refer to the tax chapter later in the book.

1 Inheriting Staff in Joint Ventures

Staff liabilities in China can be a significant overhead if not correctly assessed when either entering into a Joint Venture or acquiring part or all of a Chinese business. Here we set out the issues you need to be aware of in order not to be left with rather more than you bargained for—these situations are particularly prevalent in China's remaining state-owned enterprises.

Employee Contracts and Terms

It is important to review all employee contracts and their personnel records when inheriting staff. All staff to be taken on should be identified and checked off to ensure they really do exist, and the extent of the liabilities of employing them and the contractual terms taken into full consideration. Details of any recorded misdemeanors as well as time-keeping/productivity records should also be scrutinized.

"Ghost" Employees

It is not uncommon for someone within the company to be claiming and receiving salaries for employees who have long left the company, retired, or even died.

Check all contracts and the payroll are matched with specific, individual identification of each employee.

Qualifications and Longevity of Staff Employment

It has been known for staff that are incompetent, or with significant pension/termination liabilities to be transferred to Joint Ventures—the JV picks up this liability backdated to when the employee joined the Chinese party, and not the JV. Consequently it is possible to inherit massive termination/pension liabilities if these are not fully identified and assessed. Termination is a minimum of one month's salary for every year of service. Do you really want to be inheriting staff with 12 years' service?

Hidden Employees

Some Chinese operations "hide" their true staff overheads by making payments off the payroll to personnel. However, staff still have a legal claim as employees of the business. Ensure that the headcount and payroll match, and request a written statement from the Chinese side taking on liabilities for any staff not individually identified in any transfer of assets.

Labor Union

Make sure you have identified their charter, and payments that have been made to the Union. The business has a liability here of 2% of all staff salaries to be paid to union funds so ensure you know what this is and again that it matches up against payroll.

Pension Fund

Has this been properly administered and are the assets that should be in the fund all accounted for? You need to check with the relevant government departments that all is in order and a statement accepting retrospective liability signed off by the Chinese side.

2 Employing Chinese Staff

Yes, it may be very useful to have that ever-so-nice-and-efficient local Chinese person help you with all aspects of setting up your China operations, including all

2 Employing Chinese Staff

business licenses, offices, bank accounts, handling all documentation and so on. The language and bureaucracy are almost unintelligible and you are a busy corporate executive. But wait—is it normal business practice—anywhere—to have one person in control of all aspects of your country operations?

No, it is not. And with very good reason:

- their abilities may not stretch as far as international competencies—although they may in fact be honest and helpful, the way in which foreign companies have to be administered in China, and the reporting structures they have to go through, are very different from those that Chinese companies have to adhere to. In reality, foreign businesses in China face far more scrutiny than Chinese companies do. If your employee is not familiar with the regulatory aspects concerning operating and maintaining an international office or business in China, chances are there will be issues on which your company will immediately be out of compliance. That can, and does, get expensive. Additionally, there are circumstances where the employee may deliberately keep the company out of compliance, to obtain benefits or other leeway later if any argument arises against their favor later on.
- having one person in control of all your corporate documents and/or banking is very common. The risks are obvious. You can lose all your abilities to operate the company overnight if they decide to walk out of the door. Plus all your money.
- insertion of family and friends into your supply chain—this is very common. You need to audit your purchasing and sales departments regularly to ensure employees are not placing orders with companies owned by friends or relatives that are then charging your business at rates well over the market odds.
- setting up of parallel business—in one particularly nasty case, two employees were hired, having worked for the parent company overseas for several years, to establish a China manufacturing entity. This they did, however the China business never was able to attain anywhere like the projected sales, and had to be continuously funded from the parent to tide it over. A variety of "market conditions," "competitor pricing" and so on were given as excuses. When, just before a new US $1 million investment was to be injected into the China entity, the parent decided to have a quick internal audit, things started to become clear. The two trusted employees had established a mirror company, with a similar sounding Chinese name to the international brand, and had been diverting all orders to that business instead. "Local competitive pricing" indeed. From a business the staff themselves had established to compete with their employers.

3 Employing Expatriate Staff

There are problems with expatriate staff as well.

- hiring lawyers with no China experience is expensive and there is not really much point, especially if their Chinese language capabilities are minimal.

However, many look good, and although their firms may have a China presence, what about their individual presence in China? International lawyers are great at international work—cross border structuring and so on—but far too many of them profess expertise in areas of China practice they are neither qualified nor experienced to be dealing with. Are you looking for a salesman selling his firm, or proper advice? Really, if you need to hire a lawyer with China experience—go to a firm that has the real thing. That is what they are there for, and China has had private lawyers now for 15 years—Google their names to see how well known they are.
- hiring personnel on their language skills alone—well, everyone has to start somewhere. But a new kid just out of language school is still a new kid out of language school, and will have no experience of the "China" issues. Do not expect miracles. Two years in China does not an expert make. Young graduates do have skills of course, but do not weigh them down too much with managerial responsibilities before they have had time to adjust to a commercial business environment and have found their feet around your business. A management development program designed to take maximum advantage of their language skills yet introduce them to your business will reap greater rewards both for you and for them if you treat them with continuing educational attention.
- the China guys—expats of note are those who really know their way around, and can steer you away from all the problems we have identified here. They will have a good grasp of the language, and may well have settled down with family here. You cannot survive in China without knowing how to get on, and this is a matter of experience as well as possessing inherent patience, tenacity and people and communications skills. They are available—interestingly at this time, many of the established multinationals are localizing and expatriate engineering and other talent is perhaps more available in China than ever before.

4 Good Recruitment Practice

This applies to all staff, irrespective of nationality. Just because "this is China," there is no reason not to incorporate the normal checks and balances that you would back home.

- check language skills, both oral and written—some Chinese staff have their friends write their English CVs for them, while many expats overstate the fluency of their Chinese. Note also that regional dialects can enhance or limit the ability of your staff to operate locally
- check all backgrounds and references—often neglected. Often regretted later. Follow up those qualifications and references. You are paying for them so make sure they are really part of the package
- pay staff properly—if you want to retain them, pay them properly. Not just their welfare payments that you should be making in any event, but enough to keep them motivated and keen on continuing to work for you. China may be the

current centre of cheap manufacturing—but there is no reason for you to be cheap when it comes to your staff. Or you will end up spending more time on recruitment operations than on your actual money-making operations.

5 General Conditions and Salaries

Working hours must be in accordance with the local regulations, which normally are 8 h per day and 40 per week (if overtime is required for special reasons, it must not exceed 3 h a day and the total hours of overtime worked per month must not exceed 36 h). The company shall also cover employee's welfare, normally including pension, medical insurance, unemployment and injury. For overtime payments, the labor law states that employees must not receive less than 150 percent of their normal wage for extensions of regular working days; not less than 200 percent for extensions on days of rest and not less than 300 percent for extension of statutory holidays.

In comparing labor costs in different cities across China, please note that in more inland or remote areas workers wages are comparatively lower but, at the same time, skilled staff may also be more difficult to find.

Professional staff are constantly searching for better opportunities, living conditions and higher remuneration, so expect to pay higher salaries to retain skilled junior and middle management. Once you start developing your organization, you will also find out how high turnover could be a mounting problem to face, taking into consideration the fact that more and more companies are now rushing into the market and poaching good employees within similar industries.

The company normally provides meals. You can budget for an internal canteen or simply subcontract the provision of meals to a third party. RMB10–12 per day per person seems to be a good estimate for one employee's daily breakfast/lunch/dinner expenses. Office staff often receive a similar allowance. Please note this figure, as it will amount to quite a sum every month for larger workforces!

Manufacturing companies also normally provide lodging, so budget for around RMB50–60 per person per month. We have seen up to 16 people crammed into a tiny cubicle. Be fair to your workforce and you will gain in terms of lower staff turnover and better attitude at work. The trade unions and the local media will not hesitate to highlight poor conditions.

Mandatory Welfare Payments

When calculating salaries, pay attention to the social insurance and housing funds. These are also mandatory along with pension and unemployment funds. Some investors seem to have no idea about these, even after taking professional advice elsewhere. You need to make mandatory welfare payments to your local staff. That is the law, and you need to budget for this. How much is dependent on your location as there are variants—some of them significant—on a national basis. As a general rule of thumb it will be an amount equivalent to between 30 and 60 percent of total salaries—so you need to know exactly how to cater for this and monitor the payment of it. Not factoring this expense into your registered capital will leave you short of money, with a very unhappy labor force, and possibly legal action to recover the monies due. Pay attention to this liability and budget for meeting it.

6 The Labor Contract Law

On Friday, June 29, 2007, China's top legislature, the National People's Congress (NPC) adopted the Labor Contract Law which came into effect on January 1, 2008.

The draft, first submitted to the top legislature for deliberation in 2005 and released for public suggestions from March 20 to April 20, 2006 protects workers' legal rights by demanding a written contract. Under the current law, if employers do not sign a written contract with their employees within a year after the employees start to work for them, it should be taken as that they have signed a labor contract of an unfixed term.

It is the country's first law governing the establishment, revision, and termination of labor contracts in the People's Republic of China. It is designed to mitigate against poor working conditions, minimize labor–management disputes, and stabilize the job market. Under the previous labor contract system, employers were able to terminate contracts without notice, withhold workers' wages, and refuse to renew contracts. The current law is decidedly pro-worker, and includes many provisions that protect laborers who are in a disadvantaged position in the market economy.

Some of the key points of the law are:

Fixed Term Contracts

- a written contract between the employer and employee is required; if no contract is provided then the employment relationship will commence from the employee's first day of work. A written contract should be signed within one month of starting work, and an employer who fails to provide such a contract after one month will be forced to pay the employee twice their monthly salary.
- the law only allows for two continuous fixed-term contracts. Any further contracts must be, in general, open-term contracts

Severance Payments

- an employer must pay severance, in the amount of one month's salary for each year served, to any employee whose fixed-term contract is not renewed, unless

the employee rejects a new contract on equal or improved terms. If the employee's monthly salary is three times higher than the average monthly salary of the previous year for this region then the employer is only obligated to pay a severance equivalent to three times the average monthly salary for each year served.
- in cases of unlawful dismissal, the severance payment outlined for lawful dismissal is doubled to two months' salary for every year of service

Mass Layoffs

- employers will be required to listen to the opinions of unions and/or employees regarding mass layoffs—defined as the laying off of 20 or more employees or no less than 10% of total staff—and give 30 days advance warning, under certain specific situations provided by law, i.e. if the company has been restructured according to the bankruptcy law; or where an employer adjusts the way in which the company carries out its business, changes the nature of the business or makes technology-based changes.

Non-Competition Agreement

- employees who leave a company can be bound to a non-competition agreement for up to two years following termination, provided that corresponding economic compensation is paid to those employees on a monthly basis during the effective period of the non-competition agreement
- this may apply only for senior managers, senior technicians and other people who have knowledge of the trade secrets of the employer

Probationary Period

- The maximum probation period is based on the term of the contract, thus:
  - One month, if contract term is less than 1 year
  - Two months, if contract term is less than 3 years
  - Six months if contract term is more than 3 years
- however, where the labor contract has a specific purpose or is based on a specific project, this probationary period may not apply
- employers shall pay their employees at least 80% of their contractual salaries during the probationary period. This figure shall not be lower than the minimum salary set by the government for this particular region or provided by the employer for the same position.

Labor Unions

- the role of labor unions has been strengthened. The previous laws, which require employers to notify labor unions prior to terminating a labor contract for any reason, are still in effect. Employers that do not have established labor unions are required to notify the union at the next higher level. Unions are also allowed to engage in collective bargaining and enter into collective contracts.
- a company is required to gain approval for its employee manuals, and company rules require a consultation with the labor union, workers' congress, or by workers' representative assembly or equal negotiation, before implementation
- if the labor union or an employee is of the opinion that a rule or regulation is inappropriate then it should be improved after consultation
- the labor bureau has the right to order an employer to change company rules that violate laws and administrative statues.

China's Business Taxes

1 China's Business Taxes

On March 16, 2007 Chinese lawmakers passed the Corporate Income Tax Law, unifying the tax rates for foreign and domestic enterprises. The law, which took effect January 1, 2008, brought China's tax laws more in-line with international standards. It has unified the two existing tax codes; one for domestic enterprises, the other for foreign-invested enterprises, into one and represents a fundamental change in China's tax policy.

The Corporate Income Tax Law contains general provisions as well as chapters on what constitutes taxable income, taxes payable, tax incentives, withholding tax at the source, special tax adjustments, administration of the levy and collection of taxes, as well as some supplementary provisions.

Corporate income tax is calculated against the net income in a financial year after deducting reasonable business costs and losses – in other words it is effectively a tax on profits. It is settled on an annual basis but is often paid quarterly with adjustments either refunded or carried forward to the next year. The final calculation is based on the yearend audit.

The income tax rate for all companies in China, both foreign and domestic, is 25 percent. Industry-based tax incentives exist which reward enterprises involved in the high or new technology sectors.

Tax rate	Percentage	Applicable enterprises
Standard rate	25	Most enterprises
Reduced rate	20	Small and low-profit enterprises
Withholding income tax (WHT)	20	Foreign enterprises without permanent establishment in China but who derive income from China

Tax Incentives

A number of tax incentives exist:

- Qualified advanced technological service enterprises are eligible for a reduced income tax rate of 15 percent in 21 model cities
- "Encouraged" high-tech enterprises are eligible for a reduced income tax rate of 15 percent, irrespective of the location of such enterprises in China
- Research and development expenses can be deducted from the taxable income by 150 percent of the total amount
- More tax incentives will be granted to start-up companies, and enterprises investing in environmental protection, energy and water saving, or industrial safety
- Existing preferential tax policies for investments in infrastructure facilities, agricultural, forestry, animal husbandry and fishery industries and for those enterprises established in the western regions, have been retained

Existing tax incentives available to those qualifying enterprises which employ laid-off or handicapped workers have been replaced with super deductions applied to the wages paid to disabled employees. For CIT, the super deduction of salary paid to disabled employees is 200 percent, for IIT, monthly taxes of less than RMB2000 are exempt.

Three important tax circulars were issued in February 2008 which significantly impact foreign-invested enterprises in China. These circulars further clarified several significant areas of the corporate tax regime including tax incentives for high-technology industries and grandfathering treatments.

Circular Caishui [2008] No. 21, issued February 4, 2008, specifies tax incentives available to certain industries in the new tax law. It provides tax incentives to software production companies, IC production companies and security investment funds. These tax incentives mirror the incentives granted under the old tax regime. Preferential tax treatment will also continue to apply to IC production and assembly companies and software production companies newly established in the western region of China. Circular 21 also states that tax holidays for software production companies and IC production companies will start from the first profit-making year.

Grandfathering

Circular 21 also clarifies how the half-rate reduction during an unutilized tax holiday period should be calculated during the grandfathering period for qualifying FIEs. Circular 21 states that the half-rate reduction during the unutilized tax holiday period should be calculated based on the gradually increased tax rates of 18, 20, 22 and 24% for the years 2008, 2009, 2010, 2011 respectively, and 25% from 2012 forward. That means the net rates will be 9, 10, 11, 12, and 12.5%,

1 China's Business Taxes

depending on the year in which the half-rate reduction applies. For FIEs that were subject to a 24 or 33% tax rate under the old tax regime, the half-rate reduction during the unutilized tax holiday period should be calculated based on 25%, making the net rate 12.5%.

Old foreign enterprise income tax (%)	Transitional rate (%)	Transitional period
15	18	January 1, 2008
	20	January 1, 2009
	22	January 1, 2010
	24	January 1, 2011
	25	January 1, 2012

Circular 23 Guoshuifa (2008) No. 23, released on February 23, further clarifies aspects of the grandfathering treatments of previously enjoyed tax incentives. To qualify for reinvestment tax refunds, FIEs must have completed all reinvestment steps and obtained the dated business license of the new business license on or before the end of 2007.

For contracts involving interest or royalties that were entered into before 2008, met the criteria for withholding tax under the old tax regime, and had been already approved by the tax authorities, the withholding tax exemption will continue to apply until the expiration of the original contract. This will not apply to any extension, expansion or supplementary contract of the original contract.

Foreign-invested enterprises eligible for grandfathering treatments of unutilized tax holidays will still need to observe the original requirements stipulated under the old tax law, chief among these would be business scope and operation period. If an FIE fails to fulfill the original requirements, the tax exempted or reduced period during the tax holiday, including the part falling after 2000, would be drawn back.

Withholding Tax

Withholding tax is a PRC tax levied on overseas companies providing services to China-based businesses.

Companies based outside of China but who are supplying services to clients in China, (this can include a China-based subsidiary) your invoices are in effect "China-derived income" and the Chinese tax authorities levies taxes on these amounts. These are withheld by your client in China, being deducted from your gross invoice amount. This is why many overseas companies without a legal presence in China cannot receive the total gross amount due on their invoices to the China entity.

Your client has the responsibility of passing this tax onto the tax bureau. If they do not, or do not subtract the relevant amount of tax from your invoice, then the Chinese tax bureau will pursue the local business – and not the overseas operation – for settlement.

The withholding income tax rate for non-tax resident enterprises in China for passive income is 20 percent under the CIT law. This was reduced to 10 percent under the detailed implantation regulations of the CIT law. From January 1, 2008, this rate shall be applied to the dividends that a non-resident company receives from a resident company, unless otherwise prescribed in the tax treaty with the relevant foreign government. If the rate in the tax treaty is higher than 10 percent, 10 percent of dividends shall be adopted according to current rules; if the rate in the tax treaty is lower than 10 percent, the rate in the tax treaty should be adopted.

Tax rate on dividends from tax treaties

Tax rate (%)	Countries (regions)
0	Georgia (if the beneficial owner holds directly or indirectly at least 50% of the capital of the company paying the dividends and the total investment is no less than 2 million Euro)
5	Kuwait, Mongolia, Mauritius, Slovenia, Jamaica, Yugoslavia, Sudan, Laos, South Africa, Croatia, Macedonia, Seychelles, Barbados, Oman, Bahrain, Saudi Arabia
5 (holds directly 10% of the capital of the company paying the dividends)	Venezuela, Georgia (investment in the company paying the dividends is no less than 100,000 Euro) (10% of gross dividends if the beneficial owner holds directly less than 10% of the capital of the company paying the dividends)
5 (holds directly 25% of the capital of the company paying the dividends)	Luxemburg, Korea, Ukraine, Armenia, Iceland, Lithuania, Latvia, Estonia, Ireland, Moldova, Cuba, Trinidad and Tobago, Hong Kong, Singapore (10% of gross dividends if the beneficial owner holds directly less than 25% of the capital of the company paying the dividends)
7	United Arab Emirates
7 (holds directly 25% of the capital of the company paying the dividends)	Austria (10% of gross dividends if the beneficial owner holds directly less than 25% of the capital of the company paying the dividends)
8	Egypt, Tunisia, Mexico
10	A other cases

China has tightened its policies and procedures regarding withholding tax from non-tax resident enterprises for their China-sourced income. Non-resident enterprises with or without establishment or place in China, and those with income not effectively connected with such establishment or place, shall pay CIT on their China-sourced income. Such income includes: income from the sales of goods; income from the provision of services; income from the transfer of property, dividends and profit distribution; income from equity investment, interests, rentals, royalties; income from donation; and any other income not included in the categories listed.

The income tax payable on such income derived by non-resident enterprises shall be withheld at source, and the payer shall be the withholding agent. The withholding agent shall withhold tax from the amount of each payment that is paid or that becomes due at the time of payment or at the time the payment falls due, which means that the withholding obligation arises when such income is remitted or when the payer accrues the amount as a cost or expense under the accrual method of accounting, and the China enterprise who remits the fund overseas shall be the withholding agent.

Calculation of tax liability:

$$\text{Withholding tax payable} = \text{taxable income} \times \text{tax rate}$$

For dividends, interest, rental and royalty income, the taxable amount is the gross amount remitted before deduction of any taxes, including business tax. If the withholding tax and business tax is borne by the payer, the amount of income should be grossed up to arrive at taxable income. For dividends paid overseas, no business tax is levied. For income from the transfer of property, the taxable income amount shall be the balance of the total income amount less the net value of the property. For other income, the taxable income amount shall be calculated according to the approaches as mentioned in the preceding two items.

Administration of Withholding Tax

Non-resident enterprises subject to withholding tax in China and the China withholding agents are strongly advised to comply with the procedures to avoid potential penalties. The procedures are applied to a non-resident enterprise's China sourced dividend, interest, rental and royalty income, and income from transfer of property. The filing procedure is fairly straight forward. A copy of the contract giving rise to taxable income, along with a contract registration record for withholding income tax and other relevant documents must be submitted to the in-charge tax bureau within 30 days of signing the contract.

This procedure also applies to each subsequent revision, supplementation or extension of the contract. All documentation, including those originally in a foreign language, must be translated into Chinese. If an equity transfer is between two non-Chinese parties and the transaction takes place outside China, the resident enterprise whose equity is exchanged should file a copy of the share transfer agreement when applying for a change of its tax registration. The seller of the equity should report its taxes on its own or by appointing an agent.

The tax will be withheld from the cash payment by the payer and within seven days from the payment date, the withholding agent shall pay the amount withheld on each payment to the state treasury and submit the withholding return to local tax authorities. In the case the income is paid by installment, the withholding agent should, within 15 days before making the last payment, report to the tax bureau in charge the details of all payments already paid, together with previous withholding returns and tax payment evidence, to complete a tax withholding clearance.

The China withholding agent should maintain books and records for taxes withheld and a file of the relevant contracts, which will be subject to inspection by tax bureaus.

If the withholding agent fails to fulfill its obligation to withhold tax, non-resident enterprises shall file and pay corporate income tax to the local tax authorities where the income is derived from within seven days of the due date for tax filing and payment.

Value-Added Tax

China's value-added taxes contribute a large percentage of China's annual tax revenue and account for a significant proportion of tax liabilities for many Chinese enterprises. They affect companies that sell, manufacture, process or repair tangible goods in China and can be quite complex.

In China, VAT is administered by the State Administration of Taxation (import VAT is collected by Customs on behalf of SAT), and the tax revenue, except import VAT, is shared between the central government (75%) and local governments (25%). VAT is the major source of fiscal revenue for the government of China, particularly the central government. In 2009, the revenue from VAT amounted to RMB1.84 trillion, accounting for 31% of China's total tax revenue for the year; it accounted for the largest percentage of the China's annual tax revenues (see Table in Chap. 1).

China started to implement VAT in 1984 on 24 specified taxable item. On December 13, 1993, the State Council promulgated the Interim Regulation of the People's Republic of China on Value-added Tax ("VAT Interim Regulations") with the intent of "unifying taxation management, equalizing the tax burden, simplifying the tax system, and guaranteeing financial revenue." This law codified China's VAT system and continued to be in use until November 2008.

In 2004, China introduced VAT reforms in the provinces of Heilongjiang, Jilin and Liaoning in an effort to revitalize the old industrial base of Northeast China. The method of "increment deduction" was adopted and the scope of the reform was confined to eight industries: equipment manufacturing, petrochemical, metallurgy, automobile, shipbuilding, new- and high-tech industries, and agricultural products processing. Following the success of the pilot reform in the Northeast, it was extended in 2007 to 26 old industrial base cities in the Central Chinese provinces of Henan, Hunan, Hubei, Shanxi, Anhui and Jiangxi. In the second half of 2008, five areas of eastern Inner Mongolia and the earthquake-devastated region of Wenchuan in Sichuan Province were also designated as VAT reform pilot areas. In 2009, the central government implemented the VAT reforms nationally.

VAT Reform

On November 10, 2008, the State Council of China approved the amendments to the VAT Interim Regulations, which took effect in the beginning of 2009. The key change is a shift from a production-based VAT regime to a consumption-based VAT regime. With the exception of specific industries that the state has mandated are to be restricted, all industries in China now fall under the VAT reform system and companies are able to offset the full amount of input VAT paid on newly purchased machinery and equipment against VAT collected when they sell their products.

The main changes to the VAT Interim Regulations are as follows:

- Full VAT credit on fixed assets, but VAT-In paid on consumer goods used by taxpayers themselves (for example, cars and yachts) can't be creditable
- The VAT rate for small scale taxpayers was reduced to 3% from 4 or 6%
- Cancellation of VAT exemption policy on imported equipment for companies in "encouraged" industries
- Cancellation of VAT refund policy on purchasing domestically-manufactured equipment for companies in "encouraged" industries
- Cancellation of VAT exemption policy on imported equipment for contract processing, assembly or compensation trade

This is good news for most companies because the measures are expected to reduce the tax burden on companies. However, please be aware that this change could adversely affect cash flow in companies in "encouraged" industries as the aforementioned VAT exemption policies have been abolished. VAT exemptions on imported equipment are now gone and companies will need to increase fund reserves to pay for VAT in advance. They may also lack sufficient VAT-Out to absorb VAT-In credit (explained in detail below) on fixed assets if they export all or most of their products.

The VAT reform also presents an additional tax burden for R&D centers that imported equipment on a tax-free basis in the past. They now have to pay VAT on imported equipment under the new VAT regulation and are not able to claim any credit against their business tax liability. Companies engaged in transfer sales with local customers should note that the VAT-In paid on imported equipment cannot be refunded. In another words, it will be an additional cost under the current VAT system.

Companies may consider setting up new entities in bonded zone to alleviate the impact on cash flow as well as tax burdens arising from the cancellation of preferential VAT exemption on imported equipment as there is no VAT and customs duty on equipment imported into bonded zones.

VAT Rates

The Chinese government rules that all enterprises and individuals engaged in the sale of goods, provision of processing, repairs and replacement services, and import of goods within China shall pay VAT. There are a few exemptions, such as self-produced agricultural products sold by agricultural producers, contraceptive medicines and devices, antique books, importation of instruments and equipment directly used in scientific research, experiment and education, importation of materials and equipment from foreign governments and international organizations as assistance free of charge, articles imported directly by organizations of the disabled for special use by the disabled, and sale of goods which have been used by the sellers. However, pretty much every business will be liable for this tax.

For the sale of goods or taxable services, VAT is incurred on the date when the sales sum is received, or documented evidence of the right to collect the sales sum is obtained. For imported goods, it is incurred on the date of import declaration.

VAT on imported goods is collected by Customs on behalf of the tax authorities. VAT on articles for personal use brought or mailed into China by individuals is levied at the same time as customs duty.

VAT taxpayers are divided into general taxpayers and small-scale taxpayers, and their respective tax obligations are elaborated below.

General Taxpayer Status

According to the Measures for the Administration of the Qualification Recognition of VAT General Taxpayers enacted on February 10, 2010, taxpayers with an annual sales value not exceeding the level for small-scale taxpayers set by MOF and SAT as well as taxpayers who have newly established their business may apply to the tax department for recognition as general taxpayers.

However, full general taxpayer status is not instantly granted to wholesalers. Only after passing a three-month trial testing period as a general taxpayer under a tax officer's supervision can the wholesaler become a fully certified general taxpayer.

Taxable items	Rate (%)
Exportation of goods (except where otherwise stipulated by the state)	0
Cereals and edible vegetable oils; tap water, heating, cooling, hot air supplying, hot water, coal gas, liquefied petroleum gas, natural gas, methane gas, coal/charcoal products for household use; books, newspapers, magazines (excluding the newspapers and magazines distributed by the post department); feeds, chemical fertilizers, agricultural chemicals, agricultural machinery and plastic covering film for farming; agriculture, forestry, products of animal husbandry, aquatic products; audio-visual products; electronic publications; dimethyl ether; edible salt	13
The sales and import of goods other than those listed above; services of processing, repairs and replacement	17

VAT Calculation for General Taxpayers

The VAT rate for general taxpayers is generally 17%, or 13% for some goods (see table above). For taxpayers who deal in goods or provide taxable services with different tax rates, the sale amounts for the different tax rates shall be accounted for separately. If this is not done, the higher tax rate shall apply.

VAT payable relies on two figures: output VAT and input VAT. Output VAT is that payable on the services and goods sold by a company, namely: output VAT = A × B, where A = sales value and B = tax rate. Input VAT is that payable on the goods and services a company buys from another supplier.

The input VAT is used as a credit against the output tax levied on selling the goods. The VAT payable shall be the output VAT for the period, after deducting the input VAT for the period, i.e.:

$$\text{VAT payable} = \text{output VAT} - \text{input VAT}$$

VAT Calculation for Small-Scale Taxpayers

From January 1, 2009, the VAT thresholds for those enterprises that do not qualify for general taxpayer status have been amended. First, the sales threshold for small scale taxpayers has been reduced from RMB1 million (for enterprises engaged primarily in the production of goods or the provision of taxable services) and RMB1.8 million (for enterprises engaged in the wholesaling or retailing of goods) to RMB500,000 and RMB800,000, respectively. And second, non-enterprise units and entities that normally do not engage in taxable activities are given the choice whether or not they are taxed as small-scale taxpayers while individual (natural person) taxpayers with business turnover exceeding the threshold shall continue to be taxed as small-scale taxpayers.

The current VAT rate for small scale taxpayers is 3%. As such taxpayers cannot deduct input VAT, the formula is as follows:

$$\text{VAT payable} = \text{sales value} \times \text{tax rate}(\text{i.e., } 3\%)$$

Export Tax Rebates

Since 1985, China has had in place a tax rebate system designed to support export trade and increase the international competitiveness of companies involved in this business.

Over the past years, Chinese government has been actively discouraging the development of industries which consume high amounts of energy and natural-resources or those that pollute the environment to a great extent by lowering the export refund rates applicable to the relevant products and prohibiting the use of processing trade models.

With China's trade surplus growing rapidly, the central government has made significant changes to its VAT refund system in an attempt to slow export growth. Because of the ongoing changes to the system, export tax rebates and exemptions have now become a major cause for concern among most foreign enterprises.

As the world financial crisis took hold, the central government moved to increase the VAT refund rates on several industries in an effort to boost production. For example, China increased the tax rebate on textiles four times between 2008 and 2009. In October, 2009, the Ministry of Finance raised export tax rebates on 2,486 different types of products, an estimated one-quarter of all exports listed by Chinese customs authorities.

However, there has been a steady recovery in import/exports since 2010. In June 2010, the trend of increasing export rebate rates was reversed when the Ministry of Finance cancelled the export tax rebates for 406 products, mainly high pollution, high-energy consumption products.

So exactly what qualifies for export tax rebates? There are two important concepts to understand; the "exemption, deduction and refund" method, and the "maximum refundable amount."

The exemption, deduction and refund method and formula is generally applicable only to production enterprises qualified as general taxpayers (as noted above, there is no refund for small scale taxpayers), which are either directly engaged in export or which consign goods to other import and export enterprises for export.

Exemption, deduction and refund are defined as:

- Exemption—goods which are exported by production enterprises either directly or on consignment through foreign trade companies are exempt from VAT-Out
- Deduction—applies to enterprises whose self-produced goods are both exported (directly or through export agents) and sold domestically. The VAT-In credit on materials purchased for the production of export goods is offset against the VATOut on domestic sales
- Refund—applies if there is excess input VAT above that amount retained for credit (to be carried forward)

Exemption, deduction and refund calculation:

VAT payable = VAT-Out – VAT-In + non-refundable VAT – VAT-In brought forward from previous period

Non-refundable VAT = (export – imported free duty raw materials) × (levy rate – refund rate)

If VAT payable is a positive figure, then the enterprise will have to pay VAT to the tax bureau, if it is negative, then the tax bureau will refund the enterprise.

Maximum refundable amount calculation:

Maximum refundable amount = (collection amount from overseas for the export sales – free duty imported raw material) × refund rate

If the absolute value of VAT payable is less than the maximum refund amount, the refund amount equals the absolute value of VAT payable. If the absolute value of VAT payable is greater than the maximum refund amount, then the refund amount equals the maximum refund amount (the balance between the absolute

1 China's Business Taxes

value of VAT payable and maximum refund amount will be carried forward to the next period).

Example

Assumptions for the example are shown in the following table (in this case, we assume there is no custom duty applied).

Local purchased raw material price	300
Imported raw material price	50
Local sales price	100
Export sales price (assuming the collection has been received in current month)	400
Levy rate	17%
Refund rate	13%

Let's suppose that one-fifth of imported raw material is used for local sales based on the proportion of local sales out of total sales. The calculation of the refund amount is:

Calculation		
VAT-Out	100 × 17%	17
VAT-In	300 × 17% + 50×(1/5) × 17%	52.7
Non-refundable	[400–50 × (4/5)] × (17–13%)	14.4
VAT payable	(17–52.7) + 14.4	-21.3
Maximum refund amount	[400–50 × (4/5)] × 13%	46.8

As the absolute VAT payable is less than the maximum refund amount, the tax bureau will refund RMB21.3 to the enterprise. Note that no VAT or customs duty is levied on imported raw material used for export sales only if a company uses the Customs Handbook for importing and exporting; for imported raw material used for local sales, VAT and customs duty apply.

Profit and loss for the above case	RMB
Sales	500
Cost of raw material	350
Non-refundable VAT	14.4
Gross margin	135.6

Since the refund rate is different from the levy rate, export-oriented enterprises shall bear additional tax burdens, which ultimately will affect profit and loss.

Export Tax Rebate and Exemption Declaration Procedures

Export enterprises must follow up formal registration of tax refund to apply for a VAT refund or exemption. They should submit the following documentation to the responsible tax authority for the approval of registration, which should be obtained within 30 days from the date of export approval:

- Declaration form
- Business license
- Ministry of Commerce documentation approving export operation

After a production enterprise carries out export procedures and records the sales in their financial statement—based on the requirements of their accounting system—the enterprise can apply to the tax bureau for VAT payment and exemption and deduction, and to the same bureau for VAT refunds.

The application period for a tax refund is from the 1st until the 15th of the following month. When an enterprise applies for a VAT payment and exemption or deduction, the following documentation needs to be provided:

- Declaration of VAT payment form and other required forms
- Summary declaration form of VAT exemption, deduction and refund for production enterprise, issued and approved by the local tax refund authority
- Export invoice, import and export declaration form, export proceed cancellation and verification from the State Administration of Foreign Exchange
- Other documents as may be required by the tax authority

For newly incorporated manufacturing companies, accumulated negative VAT payable for the first 12 months cannot be refunded—this amount will be refunded in the 13th month in one lump sum. If the company cannot collect money from overseas customers for the export sales, it also cannot obtain a refund on time. If the company cannot complete the VAT effective date of registration filing for export sales within 90 days (for example: the goods are shipped outside of China and the export declaration form obtained in January, but the VAT effective date of registration filing is not completed before the end of March), these export sales must be deemed as the local sales, and are liable for 17% VAT.

Business Tax

This is a tax payable against turnover by all enterprises and individuals undertaking the following business: providing taxable services, including communications, transport, construction, finance and insurance, telecoms, culture, entertainment and service industries; transferring the provision of intangible assets; and selling immovable properties.

The basic formula is:

$$\text{Tax payable} = \text{turnover} \times \text{tax rate}$$

Only a very few items are excluded from turnover. Rates of business tax vary considerably, dependent on industry.

Business tax rates

Industry	Tax rate (%)
Transportation	3
Construction	3
Finance and insurance	5
Post and telecommunications	3
Culture and sports	3
Entertainment	5–20
Servicing agencies	5
Transfer of intangible assets	5
Sales of immovable properties	5

The Ministry of Finance and State Administration of Taxation jointly issued revised *Implementation Rules for Provisional Business Tax Regulations* on December 15, 2008, making some fundamental changes to the taxing principals of the business tax regulations. The revised rules took effect January 1, 2009.

Under the old business tax rules, the service providers were only liable to business tax in China if the taxable service was rendered within China. Thus when a foreign enterprise provided services to China clients and such services were conducted outside China, the foreign enterprise would not be subject to business tax in China. However, under the new rules, the definition of taxable services subject to business tax has been expanded to include services performed where either the service provider or the service recipient is located in China, without regard to where the service is actually been rendered. Therefore, as long as the service provider or service recipient is located in China, the service will be taxable for business tax purposes, regardless of being onshore or offshore. The only exclusion is where both service provider and service recipient are located outside China.

Financial institutions used to be subject to business tax on the trading of foreign exchange, marketable securities and futures, but non-financial institutions and individuals were not. Under the new regime, the trading of foreign currency, marketable securities, non-commodity futures and other financial commodities by any taxpayer is subject to business tax.

Formerly, deemed sales applied only to a company transferring immovable property to other parties without any consideration, however under the new rules, deemed sales apply to either a company or an individual transferring immovable property or land use rights to other companies or individuals without any consideration.

The changes in China's business tax rules have increased the amount of tax paid by multinational service providers with clients in China (see chart below). Service providers should consider modifying billing arrangements with Chinese clients by charging business tax from Chinese clients or arranging for an overseas office to bill and collect payment from their Chinese client's international affiliates if possible.

Before January 1, 2009

Scenario	Service provider	Service recipient	Service provided in China	Service provided outside	China Business taxpayer
A	In China	Outside China	Business taxable	Non-business taxable	In China service provider
B	Outside China	In China	Business taxable	Non-business taxable	Outside China service provider
C	In China	In China	Business taxable	Non-business taxable	In China service provider
D	Outside China	Outside China	Business taxable	Non-business taxable	Outside China service provider

After January 1, 2009

Scenario	Service provider	Service recipient	Service provided onshore China	Service provided offshore	China business taxpayer
A	In China	Outside China	Business taxable	Business taxable	In China service provider
B	Outside China	In China	Business taxable	Business taxable	Outside China service provider
C	In China	In China	Business taxable	Business taxable	In China service provider
D	Outside China	Outside China	Non-business taxable	Non-business taxable	N/A

Business tax is usually calculated, filed and paid to the local tax bureau every month.

When first registering for business tax, the tax bureau will issue a form showing all the taxes applicable. Businesses must be careful if they are selling goods and services simultaneously, as in these cases there are complicated criteria to judge whether business tax or VAT is applicable. Professional advice is recommended.

Consumption Tax

The current consumption tax system was introduced in 1994 along with the nationwide indirect taxes reform, including VAT and business tax. Consumption tax is levied on five categories of products:

1 China's Business Taxes

1. Products the overconsumption of which is harmful to health, social order and the environment, e.g., tobacco, alcohol, firecrackers and fireworks
2. Luxury goods and non-necessities, such as precious jewelry and cosmetics
3. High-energy consumption and high-end products, such as passenger cars and motorcycles
4. Non-renewable and non-replaceable petroleum products, such as gasoline and diesel oil
5. Financially significant products such as motor vehicle tires

This tax applies whenever certain luxury or other goods are manufactured, processed or imported. Consumption tax is levied only once. Tax rates vary considerably with the product and the tax paid is computed directly as a cost and cannot be refunded (except in rare cases upon the receipt of a consumption tax special invoice from the domestic supplier for consumption taxes paid for export goods). In addition, consumption tax is part of the base upon which VAT is levied. Be careful if you are processing taxable goods for others, since you are liable to withhold and pay consumption tax based on the value of the raw material and your processing fee. Consumption tax should be filed and paid monthly.

Consumption tax rates

Taxable items	Tax rate	Comments
Tobacco		
Grade A cigarettes	56% or RMB150 per box (250 cartons)	Includes imported
Grade B cigarettes	36% or RMB150 per box (250 cartons)	Includes imported
Cigars	36%	
Cut tobacco	30%	
Alcohol		
White spirits	20% plus RMB0.5 per 500 g/ml	Plus RMB0.5 per 500 g/ml
Yellow spirits	RMB240/ton	
Beer	Type A: RMB250/ton Type B: RMB220/ton	
Other alcoholic drinks	10%	
Alcohol	5%	
Precious jewelry and precious jade and stones	Gold, silver, platinum and diamond: 5% Other precious jewelry and precious jade and stones: 10%	Includes all kinds of gold, silver, jewelry and precious stone ornaments
Firecrackers and fireworks	15%	
Gasoline	Leaded: RMB1.4/l Unleaded: RMB1.0/l	
Diesel oil	RMB0.8/l	

(continued)

(continued)

Taxable items	Tax rate	Comments
Passenger cars, with a cylinder capacity of:		
1.5 l and below	1 l and below: 1% 1 to 1.5 l: 3%	
1.5 to 2 l	5%	
2 to 2.5 l	9%	
2.5 to 3 l	12%	
3 to 4 l	25%	
above 4 l	40%	
Small-to-medium size commercial vehicle (e.g. cross country vehicles, minibuses and vans)	5%	
Motorcycles, with a cylinder capacity of:		
250 ml below	3%	
Over 250 ml	10%	
Motor vehicle tires	3%	Radial tire exempt
Cosmetics	30%	Luxurious skin-care products are classified as "cosmetics" and are subject to consumption tax at 30%
Golf balls and equipment	10%	
Luxury watches	20%	
Yachts	10%	
Disposable wooden chopsticks	5%	
Solid wood flooring	5%	
Naphtha	RMB1.0/l	
Solvent oil	RMB1.0/l	
Lubricating oil	RMB1.0/l	
Fuel oil	RMB0.8/l	
Aviation oil	RMB0.8/l	Temporary exemption

2 Audit

All foreign-invested enterprises in China are required to prepare annual financial statements, including balance sheets and income statements for their annual Chinese audit. Such accounts must be in accordance with the Chinese accounting standards for business enterprises, irregardless of if they are foreign or domestic companies. Foreign-invested enterprises, including their legally responsible persons, must take full responsibility for the truthfulness, legitimacy and completeness of these financial statements. These documents must be completed ahead of the submission of consolidated accounts for tax purposes by the end of April every year, for the financial calendar year ending the previous December 31.

These statements will be used for computing the FIEs taxable and distributable profit. Thus, an annual audit by a firm of certified public accountants registered in the PRC is required under Chinese law.

There are a number of areas where you need to take particular care and where there are some differences between Chinese and western accounting practice. These are guidelines only, as every business is different.

Audit Items Often Queried by Chinese Independent Auditors

Adjustments for Foreign Related Payment Income

If the foreign company has paid overseas insurance for their expat employees, it should be noted that this is not tax deductible unless it is recorded as a salary payment with IIT paid. Foreign-sourced income needs to be accounted for by providing evidence of foreign taxes paid with relevant foreign documentation. Otherwise, foreign taxes may be accrued by the FIE.

Related Party Transactions and Transfer Pricing

If your FIE had any transactions with related parties, you must make sure that these were at arm's length and with adequate documentation to substantiate the charges/income, so that the results were not materially affected by related party transactions that were not in the ordinary course of business. Pay particular attention to transfer pricing issues. Tax officials reserve the right to adjust transfer prices, interest charged by related parties based on market prices or even based on the prescribed profit margin. Transfer pricing should not be used as a mechanism to reduce the amount of profit retained in China. The tax bureau regards this as tax evasion and the penalties and repercussions can be severe.

Withholding Obligations

If the FIE made or accrued in its costs or expenses any payments, royalty charges, interest, services or management fees for services performed in China by foreigners (individuals or organizations), pursuant to related contracts and agreement, the relevant withholding obligation should be provided for on an accrual basis. This means 10 percent withholding enterprise income tax and 5 percent business tax apply (the tax rate may be different according to individual cases). These charges shall be accompanied by substantial evidence—otherwise they are not deductible. All the above debts in foreign currency also need to be registered with SAFE prior to approval for remittance.

Input VAT

The VAT invoice must be verified by the tax bureau within 90 days as from the invoicing date, otherwise it cannot be deducted. Furthermore, if you have any unusual loss of inventory, then the Input VAT related to the inventory previously credited has to be reversed in the period when the loss is recognized.

VAT Refund on Export

For FIEs, VAT refunds on export should be reconciled with the tax bureau. Foreign-invested enterprises should register all export receivables of the previous year with the bureau. Failure to do so may result in the export sales being deemed as domestic transactions, subject to Output VAT if the payment for export sales is not received and related documents are not presented within the deadline.

Stamp Duty

Although not a material issue with much cost, FIEs should not forget to pay stamp duty on all books, records and applicable contracts. Fines for non-compliance outweigh the dutiable value.

3 Profit Repatriation

Your decision on planning for declaration of dividends for repatriation and/or reinvestment of profits will obviously depend on the current situation of your Chinese company and its parent company abroad, but there are a number of tax-related factors to bear in mind. This chapter introduces the procedure that must be followed when declaring dividends.

Repatriation of profits may be preferable if your organization requires the funds for re-investment abroad or return to shareholders.

Procedures for the Declaration and Repatriation of Funds

1. First of all, the amount of funds available must be confirmed. The final quarter CIT filing for the year in question will be made in early January of the following year, and after this an annual audit must be carried out. The annual

clearance process reflects the results of the audit on the accounts, and this is submitted to SAT for approval.
2. Assuming there are no problems with the submitted documents, the State Administration of Taxation will issue a tax receipt confirming the final amount of CIT payable.
3. With this figure defined, the tax payment for the year in question can be completed and the net profit figure derived.
4. Not all profit can be repatriated or reinvested. A portion of the profit must be placed in a reserve fund account. This is treated as part of owner's equity on the balance sheet. This account is capped when the amount of reserves equals 50 percent of the registered capital of the company. In addition the investor may choose to allocate some of the remainder to a staff bonus or welfare fund or an expansion fund.
5. The remaining balance is available for redistribution. Firstly, a resolution of the board of directors to authorize such redistribution must be signed by each director. Then an application form supported by the following documents must be submitted to the SAT:

- Annual audit
- Capital verification report
- Annual clearance report
- Quarterly CIT filings
- Receipts proving CIT payments have been made in full
- Bank and general details of the Chinese entity and entities receiving funds

6. SAT will review all these documents to check that everything is legitimate and issue an evidence of CIT payment certificate.
7. This certificate authorizes the bank to disperse funds as detailed on the certificate.

Note that dividends from profits made after January 1, 2008 are subject to a 10% withholding tax while those dividends connected to profits made prior to January 1, 2008 are exempt from this withholding tax. A lower withholding rate may be applicable under double tax treaties.

Joint Venture Conversions and Closures

1 Converting Joint Ventures to WFOEs

Given that no new foreign investor is being introduced, converting an existing JV to a WFOE is essentially a re-approval procedure that is reasonably straightforward to accomplish. However, the following must be taken into consideration beforehand:

- Is the industry that you are in a non-restricted activity that does not require a Chinese partner?
- Is the mechanism for purchase or transfer of shares adequately catered for in the JV articles?

Valuation of Shares and Assets

Point one is a review of the articles and a look at the mechanism for transfer. This may involve a valuation of the business, in which case both parties need to agree on this. Local valuation firms may not be entirely impartial. If you can, insist upon an independent valuer with international experience. Ideally, the preferred list of valuers should have been specified in the articles from the outset. Often there are no such articles and a board resolution to appoint a specific firm may need to be negotiated and passed.

Board Resolutions

Assuming that a price has been agreed, further unanimous board resolutions need to be passed before converting the JV to a WFOE. Usually these will tie in with an agreement over transfer of capital to purchase the equity, which then triggers the share transfer.

Re-approval

This accomplished, it is a relatively straightforward process of submitting a new set of Articles of Association, application letter and the equity transfer contract etc., to the original examining and approving authority (whichever local government approved the original JV) or the competent examining and approving authority when there is capital increase or business scope expansion, etc. These should include of course reference to the different set of laws that govern the activities of WFOEs, a new board of directors, and possibly other managerial positions as well (see our related book Setting Up Wholly Foreign-Owned Enterprises in China, for more details).

One advantage of converting JVs to WFOEs is that it may not be a requirement to inject any further capital into the business, as the JV will of course have already been essentially capitalized.

Once the new set of documents is filed, the old JV chops and licenses are handed back to the authorities and the new structure is registered as having taken its place. New chops, licenses and other pertinent certificates are issued and away you go. It is possible to keep operations intact and on-going during this process—it's not in anyone's interest for the business to have any down time as this would mean a loss of tax revenues for the local government!

Consolidated Tax Breaks

One area that can prove awkward is if this involves converting multiple JVs in different locations that have been enjoying tax breaks, but which are not in synchronization as regards time span. This will need to be negotiated with the new tax authority in the new location that will require seeing the relevant tax bureau documents from other locations prior to making a decision. Regional tax bureaus are usually fair when it comes to reevaluating multiple tax breaks and consolidating these into one—it just takes a bit of time and patience in explaining the intricacies of the previous holidays. This is an issue you may need to watch with the recent changes to the corporate income tax laws.

Acquiring Staff

Be aware that if you convert to a WFOE, your pension fund or redundancy liabilities are extended back to the time when you first formed the JV—not from day one of the converted WFOE. Have a look at your human resource issues beforehand if acquiring numerous staff—especially if having to make redundancies or planned layoffs later. It can get expensive.

Summary

Most of the problems encountered with conversion are inadequate provisions catering for this in the original articles. These of course can be amended but will need to be done beforehand to allow a smooth transition. A review is a prerequisite.

2 Liquidating Joint Ventures

The procedures for closing a JV—its dissolution and liquidation—are no easier or shorter than for the process of setting up such a company, and normally take between 6 and 9 months to complete.

According to PRC law, a joint venture may be dissolved in the following situations:

1. Termination of the duration of the venture.
2. Inability to continue operations due to heavy losses.
3. Inability to continue operations due to the failure of one of the contracting parties to fulfill its obligations prescribed in the agreement, contract and Articles of Association.
4. Inability to continue operations due to heavy losses caused by force majeure.
5. Failure to obtain the desired objectives of the operation and no prospects for future development.
6. Occurrence of other reasons for dissolution as prescribed in the contract and Articles of Association.

Upon the declaration of dissolution, the company is required to start the liquidation procedures.

For the above (2), (4), (5), (6), the board of directors should make an application to the approving authority for approval, while for above (3), the performing party is entitled to make the application.

Note also that according to the new Company Law, if a JV made a substantial loss in operation, but its Articles of Association do not provide a right to terminate in these circumstances and the shareholders or board cannot reach a unanimous resolution on termination, a minority shareholder with not less than 10% of shares may take legal action to petition for termination. Upon obtaining an order from court, the JV may proceed with liquidation and winding up.

Creation of a Liquidation Committee

1. The board will need to appoint a liquidation committee to handle the liquidation within 15 days from the dissolution date of the company.
2. The liquidation committee shall liquidate and value the company's assets in accordance with the PRC Law and the Articles of Association.
3. The liquidation committee shall consist of at least three members and the members usually should be the directors of the board. However, if the director of the board is not suitable to be the member of the liquidation committee, the liquidation committee may engage certified public accountants and lawyers.
4. The liquidation committee shall have the right to terminate employment contracts, to sell, export, transfer, assign or otherwise dispose of any and all assets belonging to the company whether they be inside or outside the PRC, as well as to conclude all business matters of the Company, in accordance with PRC Law and the principles set out in the Articles of Association.
5. The liquidation committee shall exercise the following functions and powers during liquidation:

    (a) liquidate the assets of the company, prepare a balance sheet and list of assets, and formulate the liquidation plan;
    (b) make an announcement for the benefit of unknown creditors and notify known creditors in writing;
    (c) complete any unfinished business of the company;
    (d) submit the appraisal and valuation of assets and the basis for calculation;
    (e) pay all outstanding taxes;
    (f) pay all outstanding debts in full;
    (g) settle all of the company's claims and debts;
    (h) dispose of the remaining assets after the company's debts have been settled;
    (i) represent the company in any civil litigation;
    (j) produce the Liquidation Report and submit it to the board of directors and competent approval authority for approval.

Liquidation Audits

Liquidation audits are generally required twice in the process:
- when the termination application is submitted to the related authorities and the application is approved by those authorities
- when all termination procedures have been completed.

In addition to issues covered in normal audit procedures, liquidation audits focus on these additional issues:

- the financial performance of the company for the 6 months before the date of declaring liquidation
- the completeness and truth of information on assets, such as:
  - whether the calculation of accounts receivable is correct
  - whether the bad debts write-off was properly authorized
  - whether bank account records are complete
  - whether physical assets properly belong to the company
  - whether disposal/loss of fixed assets is approved by the related authorities
  - whether investing assets are recorded and distributed correctly
  - the liabilities of the company, such as
    - whether salaries payable are calculated correctly
    - whether tax payable has been cleared properly
    - whether other liabilities have been cleared properly
    - the liquidation expenses, and whether the liquidation expenses were spent in compliance with the law.

Liquidation Deadlines

The liquidation committee shall observe the following deadlines:

- Within 15 days of beginning the liquidation, the liquidation committee must be established.
- Within 10 days of establishing the liquidation committee, the members list of the liquidation committee must be filed with the local AIC.
- Within 10 days of establishing the liquidation committee, it must notify known creditors and ask them to declare their claims.
- Within 10 days of establishing the liquidation committee, it must release an announcement in both a national newspaper and a local provincial or municipal newspaper. Within 60 days of establishing the liquidation committee, it shall make at least one additional public announcement.
- Within 180 days of beginning the liquidation, the liquidation report must be submitted to the approving authority.
- Within 10 days of submitting the liquidation report, the liquidation committee should perform the deregistration procedures with tax and customs authority and receive the corresponding statements.

Distribution of Liquidated Proceeds

In accordance with PRC Law, revenues from the sale or disposal of the liquidated assets shall be paid out in the following order:

- liquidation expenses, including expenses for management, sales and distribution for liquidation, expenses for announcement, lawsuit and arbitration, remuneration to members of and advisors to the liquidation committee and other expenses occurred during the liquidation
- wages, labor insurance premiums and welfare benefits of employees
- outstanding taxes
- outstanding secured debts
- other outstanding debts.

After payments have been made in accordance with the provisions above and upon completion of the liquidation procedures, the remaining revenue shall be distributed to the shareholders according to the ratio of capital contribution.

Cancellation of Registration

Upon completion of the liquidation procedures, the liquidation committee shall submit the Liquidation Report, approved by the board, to the approval authority, and return its business license and cancel its registration with the relevant government authorities including the Ministry of Commerce, SAIC, the customs administration, the taxation authorities and SAFE. All the company's bank accounts shall be closed. The accounting books and other documents of the JV should be kept by the Chinese shareholder.

Within 10 days from submission of the Liquidation Report, the company should perform deregistration with the authorities, and upon completion of the deregistration, the company can repatriate the remaining funds back to the investor. The deregistration includes:

- deregistration from the MOFCOM, and cancellation of the Approval Certificate
- tax audit and deregistration from the local tax bureau
- tax audit and deregistration from the state tax bureau
- customs deregistration
- deregistration with the State Administration of Foreign Exchange (SAFE)
- deregistration from the State Administration of Industry and Commerce (SAIC)
- deregistration of the Business Code Certificate
- public announcement in a newspaper to terminate the business
- remit funds back to investors
- close bank accounts.

Glossary of Terms

AIC	Administration of Industry and Commerce
BOFTEC	Bureau of Foreign Trade and Economic Cooperation (local approvals authority)
CIT	Corporate Income Tax
CJV	Co-operative Joint Venture
EPZ	Export Processing Zone (state-level)
EJV	Equity Joint Venture
ETDZ	Economic and Technological Development Zone (state-level)
FDI	Foreign Direct Investment
FICE	Foreign-Invested Commercial Enterprise
FIE	Foreign-Invested Enterprise
FTZ	Free Trade Zone (state level)
HIDZ	Hi-Tech Industrial Development Zone (state-level)
IIT	Individual Income Tax
JV	Joint Venture
M&A	Merger and Acquisition
MOFCOM	Ministry of Commerce
MOF	Ministry of Finance
NDRC	National Development and Reform Commission

PRC	People's Republic of China
RMB	Renminbi (Chinese currency unit, also know as Yuan)
RO	Representative Office
SAFE	State Administration of Foreign Exchange
SAIC	State Administration of Industry and Commerce
SAT	State Administration of Taxation
SETC	State Economic and Trade Commission
SEZ	Special Economic Zone (state level)
VAT	Value Added Tax
WFOE	Wholly Foreign-Owned Enterprise
WTO	World Trade Organization